THE AMERICAN CHARACTER

THE AMERICAN CHARACTER

Norman Vincent Peale
with
William Thomas Buckley

WYNWOOD™ Press
New York, New York

Library of Congress Cataloging-in-Publication Data

Peale, Norman Vincent, 1898-
The American character / Norman Vincent Peale.
p. cm.
ISBN 0-8007-1605-1
1. National characteristics, American. 2. Interviews – United States. I. Title. 88-15306
E169. 12. P43 1988 CIP
920' .073 – dc 19

Published by WYNWOOD™ Press
New York, New York
Printed in the United States of America

CONTENTS

INTRODUCTION

Americans are good people. The experience of a lifetime convinces me that this is a true observation.

Admittedly, we Americans have problems that regularly occupy (some might say *pre*occupy) the news media. Yet I'm persuaded that tales of greedy, corrupt, selfish and uncaring individuals are a distinctly secondary part of our story.

Over the years, I have met and spoken with many thousands of Americans—some famous, most little known. And in the course of conversation, they have indicated time and again, in diverse ways, that Americans are idealistic believers in the good, that goodness is intrinsic to the American Character.

Folks don't often come right out and say "Americans are good people" in so many words; they usually tell a story or recall an experience that reflects the point.

Nevertheless, the positive features that they see as ingrained American traits – the ones they prize in themselves and others – are unmistakable: courage, grit, heroism, perseverance, honesty, generosity, compassion, charity, loyalty, selflessness, dedication, neighborliness, and decency – the determination to "do what's right."

And Americans are a faith-inspired people — possessed of a deep, abiding belief in God who strengthens them, sustains them, guides them. Religious conviction has always held a crucial place in our national heritage from the very beginning, since religious conviction was among the principal motivators for the Plymouth colonists who sought, among other things, the freedom to worship God as they saw fit. In America they found that freedom, as did those who came after them. Americans over the centuries have practiced their religious beliefs in many ways, in virtually all languages, in every sort of cathedral, church, temple, synagogue, and house of worship. Yet despite this diversity, faith has not been a dividing force, but a unifying one: It has made us "one nation, under God" – a people sharing a common regard for the God-inspired qualities that give us our purpose and identity.

I have learned through the years that many of the unassuming Americans I've encountered on a day-to-day basis have known these uplifting qualities firsthand, having themselves performed stirring acts of bravery, self-sacrifice, caring and good-neighborliness. Had these people been famous, their experiences might have entered our national folklore, like Washington's truthfulness or Lincoln's honesty. But because they were obscure citizens, their stories often weren't widely told. And to me, this always seemed a waste, an opportunity lost to inspire others.

So it was that I welcomed an invitation a few years ago from broadcast producers John and Gloria Scott and Howard Greene to take part in a radio series they were creating that was dedicated to revealing and cultivationg the positive, the upbeat, the good side of American life. This nationwide program, called "The American Character," appeared daily on several hundred radio stations for most of a decade, thanks to the public-spirited support of the ITT Corporation, which was from the start the sole funder of these commercial-free broadcasts

From untold hours of interviews exploring the experiences of more than two thousand people in all walks of life, "The American Character" developed a picture highlighting the features and traits that distinguish the best aspects of our national life. It was this picture, in true stories about contemporary people, that the radio series presented.

Owing to the nature of radio, however, the image was necessarily fleeting, depicting on any one occasion only a small portion of the overall American panorama.

But with this book, the opportunity is at hand to draw upon the rich resources of our radio chronicles and to share, in one place and at one time, the grand portrait of "The American Character"– illustrated through the real-life experiences of everyday citizens whose deeds fill our hearts with pride and ennoble the meaning of what it is to be an American.

THE AMERICAN CHARACTER

THE LAND

**My country, 'tis of thee,
Sweet land of liberty,
Of thee I sing:
Land where my fathers died,
Land of the pilgrims' pride,
From every mountainside
Let freedom ring.**

SAMUEL FRANCIS SMITH
America

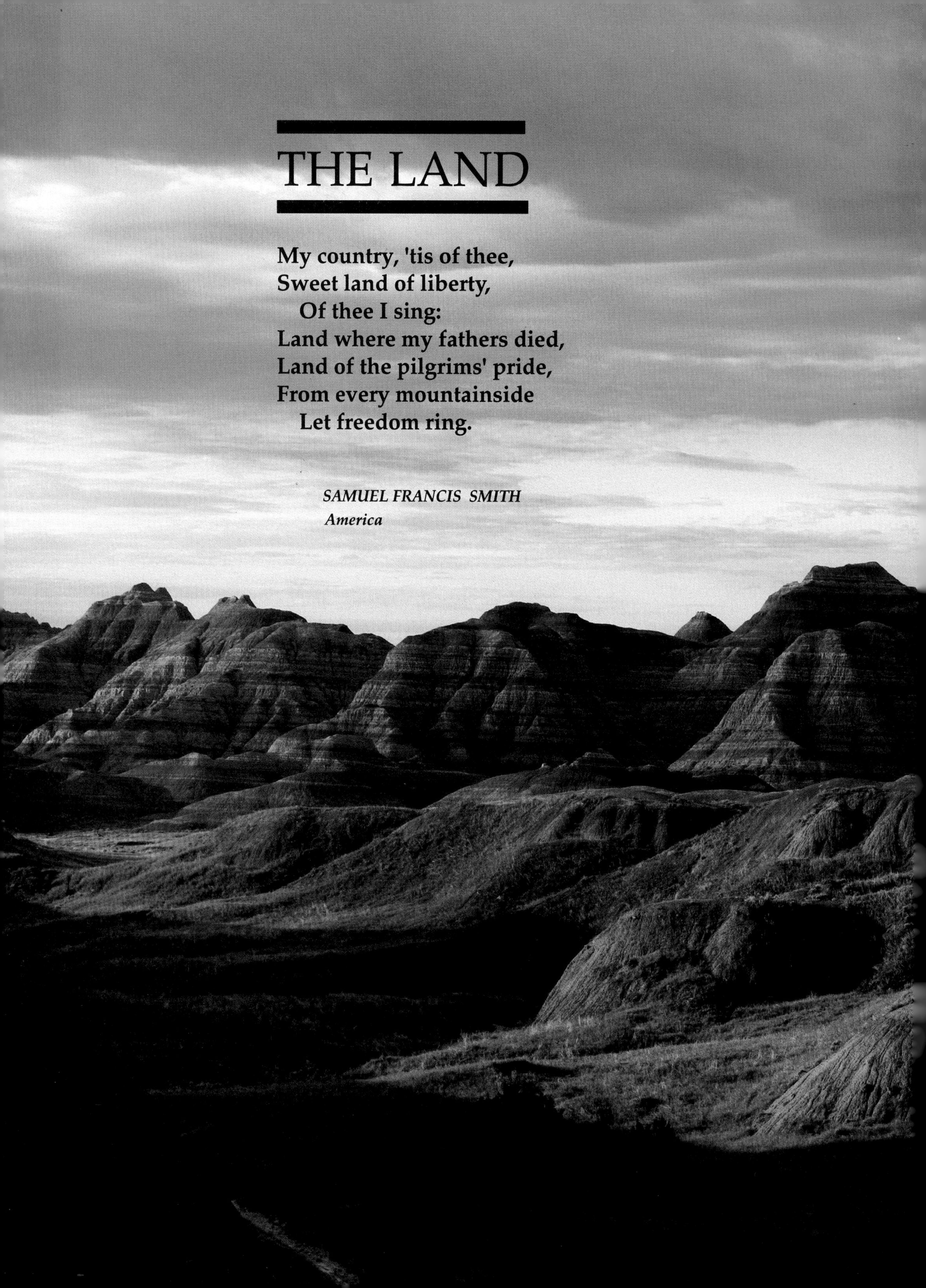

LAVERNA GAIL

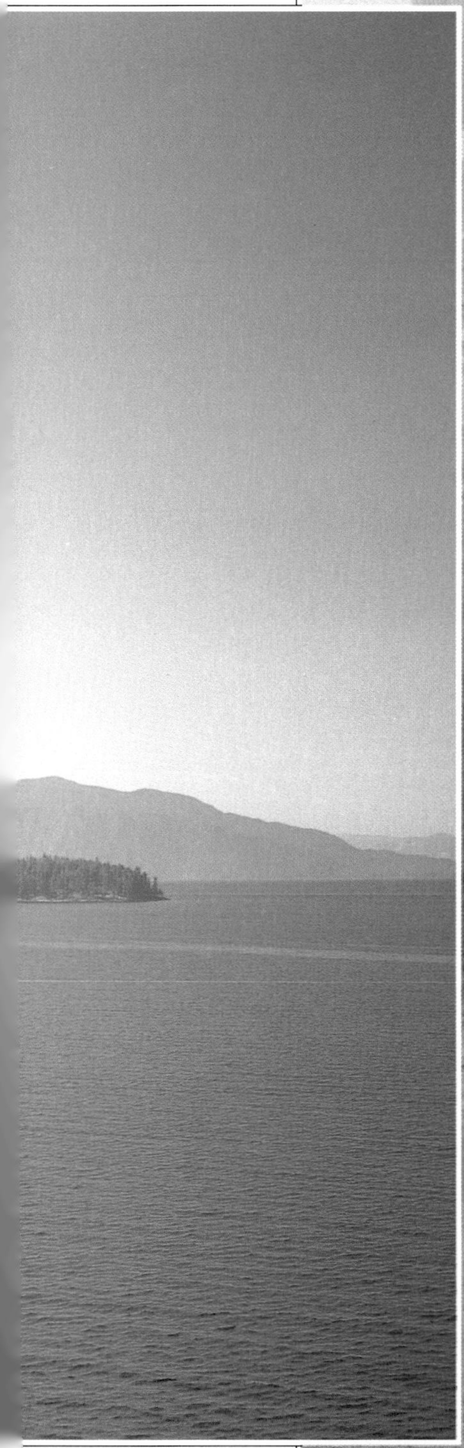

HEROISM

Examine the foundations of American life and you will discover heroism laced through and through, like rods of steel in reinforced concrete. Heroism is the stuff on which this country was built.

The pages of our history are thick with the exploits of heroes, and no era has been without them, be they the courageous Pilgrims, the daring frontier pathfinders, the sturdy settlers of the westward movement, the gallant men and women of our military struggles, the geniuses of scientific and technological advancement, the achievers of industry and commerce, the leaders of government and politics, the luminaries of sports and entertainment.

But what is heroism? About this, there are varied opinions. Stop a dozen individuals on the street and you'll get a dozen definitions of heroism, no two just alike, because heroism means different things to different people. Many think of heroism as life-risking physical courage. Others see it in excellence of performance or achievement. Still others insist it must reflect nobility, sacrifice, and selflessness. Some perceive heroism in people's ability to inspire the best in those around them. Not a few see heroism in folks who do their jobs, raise their families, discharge their responsibilities, and pass their lives quietly and decently.

Heroism, then, is like beauty: It is in the eye of the beholder. So look upon the Americans whose stories follow; behold heroism in the American character.

John Kohl

John Kohl (left) receiving the Carnegie Award for heroism.

Christopher Kohl.

Though the actions of John Kohl, from Northumberland, Pennsylvania, spoke unmistakably of heart-stopping gallantry, the lingering echoes that surrounded him whispered unforgettably of compassion and selflessness.

John, forty-two, was a brakeman who had worked on the railroads for more than half his life. Yet for all his long experience, he had never encountered anything like the scene that met his eyes one day as he peered from the locomotive of a Conrail freight train rolling up the slopes of the Allegheny Mountains near Altoona, Pennsylvania. As the train rounded a bend at twenty-five miles an hour, John made out a "dark spot" on the tracks about a thousand feet ahead. He assumed it was one of the small animals that often strayed onto the tracks in that area, so the train crew did as they'd always done in such cases — they gave a blast on the horn.

"The spot moved," John remembered. "It stood up. It wasn't an animal. It was a child!"

With a heart suddenly turned acrobat in his chest, John screamed at the youngster to get off the tracks as the engineer leaned on the diesel horn.

"But the little girl did just like the little animals do," John said. "She tried to run away from us, straight up between the rails."

John and the engineer had both tripped the emergency switch at the same instant, locking all brakes on the three-locomotive, sixty-two-car train. It began slowing down. But it was clear that the lumbering giant would never stop short of the child, who, exhausted and terrified, had plopped down on the tracks, sobbing. The brakeman knew he hadn't a second to spare.

"I jumped onto the running board and climbed to the outside front of the engine, where a snowplow was mounted — kind of like an old-fashioned cowcatcher," he said.

"I hooked my left leg over the plow. My right foot was on the bottom step of the ladder that went up to the engine. With my right hand, I held onto a grab-iron. So I was hanging out there in front of the locomotive with my back to the ground, maybe two feet above the tracks, with my left hand free. The little girl was sitting on the rail nearest me, crying. I had my head twisted around and was looking right into her eyes. I could see the fright. I had my eyes fixed on her, watching her all the time. We were bearing down fast."

At this point, John stretched out as far as he could in front of the train; like a first baseman straining to make the big play. For John Kohl, this was to be the play of a lifetime.

"I was able to extend maybe three or four feet ahead of the engine. We were just about on top of her when I gave this sort of upsweep with my free hand and flipped her off the rail," he recalled. "She landed on her belly a couple of feet away. I started hollering for her to stay down, stay down. The way she

Sounds of gallantry, echoes of compassion.

was looking toward the tracks, I thought she might get all confused and run underneath the cars. But she stayed put and I hit the ground running, without waiting for the train to stop." It rolled on more than four hundred feet before finally coming to a halt.

"Me and the conductor ran back and found the girl very scared, crying. She looked maybe eighteen months, two years old. I picked her up and held her tight against my right shoulder. She wrapped her arms around my neck and hugged me, real hard. After we walked a little way, she stopped crying.

"I carried her over into a small parking lot where I saw some people. It was her mother and father, who'd been looking for her. They walked towards us, then hesitated. Her mother didn't say anything — couldn't say anything. She was in shock, speechless. She thought the child was hit, maybe dead."

Less than a year earlier, John and his wife, Judy, had not been as fortunate as these breathlessly anxious parents. The Kohls had received the sudden news that their son, Chris, who was seventeen, had been killed in a farm accident. Now, having saved the life of this little girl named Jeanne, who was just twenty-two months old, John drew comfort from the realization that he'd spared her family the grief his family had known.

People made a lot of fuss over John Kohl's daring rescue of the child, but the railroad man remained characteristically modest. "I'm glad I did what I did, but as far as heroism or anything like that, I don't feel that way. Anyhow," John observed, "being a hero isn't something you say about yourself. It's something that other people say about you."

What other people said about John was typified by the recognition he received from the Carnegie Hero Fund Commission, which honored him with a hero's medal and a $2,500 reward, presumably closing the book on his gallant story.

But John Kohl's story was far from over, for he and his family felt a special bond, a kinship, between themselves and the young life John had saved at the risk of his own on the tracks outside Altoona. The Kohls wanted this attachment to endure. So with proceeds from John's Carnegie award, they set up a trust fund that would reach maturity in just about sixteen years, on the eighteenth birthday of its beneficiary: a little girl named Jeanne.

 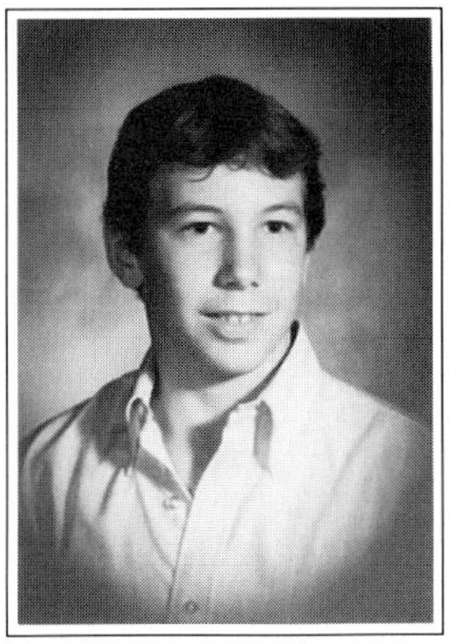

Wendy and Andy Plagman

Though it may be comforting to imagine that heroes fear nothing — that they rise above the average plane of mortality to perform their admirable deeds without misgiving — this notion is more fancy than fact. Heroes, too, feel the hot breath of danger; they also are afraid. What sets heroes apart is not their absence of fear, but their mastery of it.

Teenager Wendy Plagman would be the first to admit that she was anything but fearless when a bull went berserk and attacked her uncle on his farm outside Elkader, Iowa. Yet the fear she felt didn't keep her from trying to save his life at the risk of her own.

Wendy, fourteen, was watching as her uncle, LaVerne Plagman, went inside the pen of a three-year-old bull to set the beast loose.

"The animal just went mad and turned on me," LaVerne recounted. "He had me down before I could move, butting me and pounding me. I couldn't get away."

Immediately, Wendy and LaVerne's fourteen-year-old son, Andy, began shouting and waving to distract the bull, which fortunately had no horns. This strategy worked briefly, but after a few moments the animal turned back toward LaVerne.

Andy tried to protect his dad by taking a pitchfork to the bull and thrusting it into the animal's neck. However, this only seemed to incite the brute, which gave one flick of its head and tore the pitchfork out of Andy's grasp as though it were a table fork. Then the rogue went after LaVerne more furiously than ever, battering the defenseless man and eventually rooting him off the floor and hurling him ten feet through the air, knocking him unconscious.

LaVerne's life might well have ended right there, under the pounding head and hooves of the rampaging bull. Many a cattleman had died just that way. But it was not to be LaVerne's fate.

Leaping into the enclosure, Wendy Plagman confronted the crazed animal in a classic mismatch: a five-foot-tall, 110-pound girl against one ton of angry beef.

"I didn't have a plan," Wendy confessed. "I didn't know what I was going to do until I saw him knock the pitchfork out of Andy's hands. I picked it up and started stabbing the bull in the shoulder and neck, and then right in the nose."

At this point, LaVerne regained consciousness. "I came to," he said, "and saw Wendy standing between me and that bull. She had him backed into a corner, facing him down with a pitchfork. I managed to get on my feet and close the gate."

It was then that LaVerne, fifty-one years old, began feeling the effects of the attack. "I was in awful pain," he remembered. "They put me in intensive care at the hospital. My ribs were broken. Muscles were torn in my arm and shoulder. My leg was squashed. I was black-and-blue from the top of my shoulders to the soles of my feet. The docs told me I was bruised just as bad on the inside as the outside, but thankfully only the ribs were broken."

Even so, it took LaVerne over a year to recover from his injuries, which were not the first this bull had caused. Wendy recalled an earlier encounter with the animal. "He had gone after me once a few months before that," she said. "He butted me real hard with his head and hurt me — hurt my arm and ribs. After that, I stayed out of his way. I was afraid of him."

Nevertheless, when her uncle's life was threatened, Wendy Plagman mastered her fear. She challenged the ominous beast, eye to eye. And she did not blink.

Ed Sprissler

Ed Sprissler leaning over his butcher counter, helping kids cross the street, and a drawing from one of "his kids." (Photos © Norman Y. Lono/Philadelphia Daily News.)

The efforts of Philadelphia butcher Ed Sprissler represented a different kind of heroism, the sort that might be described by the word "everyday." Because to hundreds of kids, Ed *was* a hero every day — every *school* day — of their lives. He earned their respect and affection with the unselfishness and concern that mark decent men.

Ed had a butcher shop in the Olney section of Philadelphia near the corner of Fourth and Spencer, an intersection busy with the rush of automobiles and the tramping feet of schoolchildren. It was the mingling of these two forces — cars and kids — that troubled Ed. "There were stop signs, but a lot of drivers somehow ignored them," he explained, "and I used to see these really little kids trying to get across the street, darting through traffic, dodging cars.

"That got me a little excited. My heart would be in my mouth a couple of times every morning; it got so I couldn't stand the taste," he said. "So one day I went out there and started helping the kids across. And I sort of stayed with it."

It was an unsolicited responsibility that he stayed with for the better part of a decade, purposely going to work and opening up his shop a half hour earlier than necessary every day so he could keep an eye on the more than five hundred kids who crossed Fourth and Spencer on their way to school.

"I didn't try to control the traffic. I controlled the kids, instead — held them back until it was clear to cross. I was like a safety-patrol boy, and my butcher's apron was the uniform of the day," he laughed.

With his silvery hair and smile-creased face, Ed, who had eight grandchildren of his own, became every kid's grandfather, watching over them, joking with them, being a friend to all of them. "I'd coax them, kid them, jolly them along," he recalled with a chuckle, "to make sure they always got to school on time."

Then one day, Ed Sprissler's time on the corner came to an end: He hung up his apron and retired. But he never deserted. He didn't leave Fourth and Spencer until the city of Philadelphia posted an official, salaried crossing guard there.

Juli Cullison

To triumph over fear alone, Juli Cullison would need courage. She had courage. To triumph over pain alone, she would need toughness. Juli also had toughness. But fear and pain *together*; what would she need to triumph over these? Whatever it was, she had that, too.

Eight-year-old Juli showed what she had one bitter winter's morning near Crawford, Colorado. She was riding to school with her sister, Jennifer, and their parents, Gill and Donna Saunders, when their car hit a patch of ice, flipped, and landed on its top.

Juli and her mom were thrown clear, but the vehicle came to rest on Gill and ten-year-old Jennifer, trapping them. Jennifer was bloodied and badly hurt, while Gill seemed uninjured, though he couldn't move.

Wrecked at the side of a remote country road in the heart of the Rockies with the temperature hovering at zero, the family was desperate for help. But they could not wait for it to come to them. If aid were to arrive in time, Juli or her mom would have to fetch it. Which of them would go?

"I thought I should stay and take care of Jennifer's bleeding," said Donna. "I also was concerned that the wreck might catch fire, which Juli couldn't be expected to handle. To top everything off, I was eight months' pregnant — in no condition for a hike. I decided to send Juli. I asked her if she was okay, and she said she thought so," Mrs. Saunders recounted. "So I told her, 'You've got to go bring help.'

"Juli said, 'But I'm afraid, Mama,' and I told her, 'If you can, you must.' She said she would try. I watched her go, not suspecting that it would be her last walk for over three months."

Hurrying as fast as her short legs would carry her, Juli set off down the road toward where she thought a farm was located.

"I was afraid of losing my way, and scared of being alone," the child would later recall. "I never walked on the open road by myself before, never in my life. This was the first time, because Mama never allowed us."

Cold and lonely, Juli pressed on.

"After I walked for a ways, my back got real sore," she said. "Then I started hurting all over, in my hips and legs and back. I felt like I should lie down, but I knew I couldn't. I had to keep going, or I wouldn't be in time to get help.

"It seemed like I walked twenty miles, but it was probably less than a mile," Juli said. Eventually, she reached a farmhouse. "When I knocked on the door and no one answered, I got scared again. Then I heard a tractor and waved for help."

A kindly farmer spotted Juli and responded to her gesturing. He got his car, put Juli in the backseat, and drove to the accident scene. "When we got there, I was lying down," Juli said. "I tried to sit up, but couldn't. I had too much pain."

A hydraulic jack was used to remove Gill and Jennifer safely from the wreck. Then the entire family set out for the nearest hospital, thirty-five miles away.

Astonished doctors there could not believe their eyes or ears when they examined Juli and heard the story of her trek for life. It was beyond their imagining how she could have managed to walk so much as one block, not to mention most of one mile. After all, they noted, the child had an ankle that was badly injured, a leg that was severely punctured, a back that was dislocated, and a pelvis that was fractured in two places! In that condition, the doctors agreed, it should have been impossible for her to walk.

Nevertheless, she had walked. And walked. She persisted until her goal was reached, her duty was done, her family's safety was assured. Then she collapsed.

Juli remained in the hospital for fifteen days and was bedridden at home for three months. Although she largely recovered from her injuries, she was still undergoing surgical correction of their effects more than three years after the accident.

If Juli Cullison's triumph over fear had equaled courage, and her triumph over pain had equaled toughness, what then of her triumph over fear *and* pain? In one so young, that had no equal.

Steve Edmonson

It seemed at first that Steve Edmonson's tenderness and sensitivity contradicted his reckless, raw-edged bravery. Later, though, it became clear that these gentle traits didn't contradict his bravery: They motivated it.

The two sides of Steve's character surfaced during a few harrowing moments at a weigh station on Interstate 85 outside La-

Grange, Georgia. Steve, thirty-one, who lived in nearby Manchester with his wife and two small children, was at work as an enforcement officer for the Georgia Department of Transportation when somebody hollered that a tractor trailer parked outside the station was on fire.

Knowing that there were several eighteen-wheelers in the lot, Steve dropped what he was doing and ran outdoors. His pulse quickened when he saw which of the trucks was smoking.

Earlier that day, the big, soft-spoken Georgian had investigated that very rig after its driver was arrested by police and taken away, leaving his family waiting for him in the sleeper-equipped vehicle. Steve remembered seeing a woman in the cab of the truck, holding a little boy on her lap. Later, minutes before the fire was spotted, Steve had noticed the same woman waiting to use the telephone. She was standing in line alone, *without* the child!

"Other than the woman herself, I guess I was the only one who knew there must be a young one in that truck," said Steve. "Nobody else *could* have known, because it was impossible to see anything inside there. The smoke was so heavy, it was like somebody had taken paint to the windows. They were completely blacked out."

Worse than being unable to see inside, Steve couldn't get inside. The doors were locked and the windows tightly closed.

"I jumped up on the truck and drew back my fist to break the window," recalled Steve, a powerful man who stood six-foot-two. "But I stopped myself because it occurred to me that the boy might be right on the other side. I thought flying glass could hurt him as much as smoke.

"So I pressed open a vent window and reached in for the door handle, but I couldn't locate it. I did find the window crank and began turning. That's when the flames started up. It was like a big vacuum, sucking in air and blowing out fire.

"I was looking into this blackness, seeing nothing. I knew I had to go in there, though, and I was scared to death. No doubt about it. I was the scaredest man in the world right then — scared I wouldn't be able to find that little boy."

Steve paused for a long moment as his daughter, Baylee, and son, Drew, played noisily in the background, then he continued.

"I closed my eyes and climbed through the window. I couldn't see, or breathe, or nothing. Couldn't even open my eyes, the smoke was so bad. I just started grabbing and sweeping. After a few passes, I snagged the little boy and put him through the window," Steve recounted. "I stuck my head outside and started to leave when the fire kind of exploded — flared up — and pushed me out onto the ground.

"Laying there on my back in the parking lot, I remember thinking that I'd done it, I'd saved the boy. Then I saw the woman, the child's mother, running toward the truck, screaming, 'My baby's in there. My *other* baby's still inside!' Of course, I didn't know there was more than one child. All I'd ever seen was one."

But there were two little boys: the three-year-old he'd just rescued, and another, twenty-three months old, still inside the tractor.

Steve had already taken a big chance in dangerous circumstances. Would he do the same again, now, under even worse conditions?

"I had to," he explained. "I knew I couldn't face myself if I didn't at least try, no matter what the outcome might be. I heard people hollering that the fuel tanks could blow or the top of the cab might collapse," he said. In fact, by the time the fire eventually burned itself out, the tractor was reduced to molten junk, with nothing left except the frame and wheels. "But none of that mattered, because I'd made my mind up to get that child out, and there wasn't nothing going to stop me, even if I *was* thinking to myself, *Nobody could be alive inside there. It's impossible. All you're going to find in there is bones.*"

For the second time in as many minutes, Steve Edmonson plunged into the hellish inferno, wagering his life against the uncertain chance of saving a life that might already have been lost.

"The inside of that cab was like a furnace. Flames coming from overhead and the floorboards on the passenger side. I held my breath, squeezed my eyes shut, and felt around," he said. "The lady screamed that the baby was probably in the sleeper, behind the driver's seat, but there wasn't nothing there.

"I was the scaredest man in the world...."

"Something told me to check the driver's-side floorboards. I started poking around down there, and then I felt something. It was him. The boy done had hisself wedged between the door and the driver's seat. I snatched him up quick and put him through the window."

Scrambling to safety, Steve's eyes fell on the two children he'd just taken from the burning truck. When he saw their condition, his elation turned to despair; his heart sank.

"Earlier, when I noticed the first boy sitting in the truck on his mama's lap, he was the prettiest little blond-haired kid you ever saw. Now, he was solid black from top to bottom — hair, face, even mouth and teeth.

"I thought at first he was dead," said Steve, who had seen other burn victims during several years as a Manchester fireman. "He wasn't, though. So while we waited for the ambulance, I took him and tried to do what I could to clean him up and cool him off. He was conscious but couldn't manage to say much. He kept calling, 'Daddy, Daddy. Where's Daddy?'"

At the hospital, the little boy died. And even though the lad's younger brother recovered fully because of one man's courageous gamble, years later, Steve Edmonson remained tortured by thoughts of what might have been.

"I still dream about it. It's in my mind sometime every day, some way or another," Steve confided. "I wonder maybe if I'd been a little faster, or maybe if we'd gotten him to the hospital sooner, maybe he'd have lived. What bothers me the most is thinking about how much pain that little boy went through. I know how hot it was in that truck; remember, I felt a little bit of the heat that he felt.

"When I looked into the smoke and fire, I thought, *That could be Drew and Baylee in there.* My kids were just about the same ages as those two. In my mind, those two little boys *became* mine. At that moment, they belonged to me, were my personal kids, and it was up to me to get them out.

"Some people thought my fire training accounted for my actions. But that's wrong. Fear was responsible. Fear of the situation. Fear of what might happen to those kids. Fear that they would suffer. Especially that: fear of them suffering. Because kids should never have to suffer for anything or ever be hurt in any way. They only ought to be held and spoiled and loved."

Fear and bravery, dread and daring, tenderness and recklessness abided side by side in Steve Edmonson's heart. Understanding that can't explain how he did what he did. It can explain why.

Casey Cannon at the piano.

Casey Cannon

A golden thread intertwining all heroes is something that we who recognize them see in them: reflections of ourselves. In touching our lives with their actions, our heroes inspire us, help us to see ourselves becoming more than we are, by becoming more like they are.

Casey Cannon of Ellington, New York, was a hero to everyone whose life she touched. Indeed, it was difficult to imagine anyone's not wanting to be like Casey in almost every way. She was intelligent, enthusiastic, brimming with good cheer, filled with the joy of living, and possessed of a musical talent bordering on genius.

Given all of this, plus loving parents and two doting big brothers, one might have been tempted to say that nine-year-old Casey "had it all." She hadn't, though, for Casey came into the world perfect in every way save one: She was born blind.

"When Casey was diagnosed, we were crushed," said her mother, Jackie. "We had two beautiful boys and now this lovely little girl who couldn't see. It was difficult to accept; it was depressing."

The Cannons' despair began to lift after a few months, however, with the realization that aside from her lack of vision, Casey was entirely normal — which was not to say ordinary. Before long, she showed herself to be in many ways extraordinary.

For example, Casey reflected unusual brightness when she contrived to master the art of crawling — backwards! This spared her countless lumps on the head from bumping into furniture if she crawled forwards. She was quick to talk and was spelling words when she was only three.

The most thrilling revelation, however, came when Casey, at the age of two, sat at a piano and without prompting began to play melodies from her nursery rhymes. One Sunday, she heard "Amazing Grace" at church, then went home and performed it for her family. Before long, it was a game: Let her hear a tune once, and her pudgy little fingers would find it hidden in the keys of the piano. She began taking lessons at three. Her twin ambitions became playing both Carnegie Hall and the "Muppet Show." By the age of five, this dimpled, pigtailed, smiling delight was giving recitals of Bach preludes, assorted children's songs, and some of her own brief compositions — with equal parts of talent and courage. She embraced both audience and keyboard without hesitation.

Casey was no less courageous away from the piano. When she went off to school, she "mainstreamed," attending regular classes just like the other kids, becoming the only blind student in her school district. Math and a lack of Brailled books posed obstacles, but she overcame these as she did all other obstacles: cheerfully, optimistically, bravely.

In her education as in her music, Casey grew to be almost as much teacher as student, opening eyes and minds and hearts to the possibilities of her positive attitude. "Casey doesn't believe there's *anything* she can't do if she puts her mind to it," said Jackie, "and she affects other people much the same way.

"Recently, a high school girl who'd been working with Casey on a computer Brailling project confided in me. The girl said she'd known all along that she was going to college but hadn't known what she was going to study. But now, she said, 'Because of Casey, I know what I want to do with my life. Meeting her and seeing her happy approach to everything, I want to go into special education and teach handicapped children.' Think of it," said Mrs. Cannon, "this girl's life was changed just by knowing Casey. I felt so good about that I cried."

For Jackie, those weren't the first tears shed on Casey's account. In the beginning, tears had been an everyday occurrence. "I used to cry over her blindness," said Jackie. "I knew that the Bible said there is a reason for everything. But why this? There was no way in the world I could imagine a reason why our beautiful baby daughter couldn't see. I prayed. I cried. I prayed. But even when Casey showed a talent for music, I still couldn't make out anything in the way of a 'reason.'

"Then slowly, gradually, I came to see the reason, to understand why Casey was born blind," Jackie explained. "Why? Because if she'd had sight, even with her terrific piano ability, she wouldn't have touched nearly as many people as she has. Casey has reached so many lives that it's unreal. I've been to all of her recitals and have read all the grateful notes and letters she's received, but still I have a hard time comprehending how many troubled lives she has touched and helped. Who knows how many others she has inspired and given hope to?"

Or how many more in the future?

Jim Patridge with Jennifer Kroll.

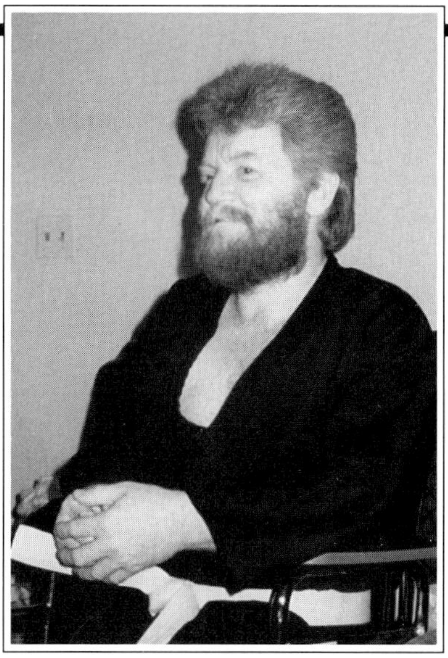

Jim Patridge

Heroism can visit a man in many unexpected ways. Jim Patridge knew some of them.

He could recollect, for instance, the unexpected events of a June day that found him puttering around his house in West Chicago, Illinois, when the suburban calm was pierced by one hair-raising scream. Then another. And another.

They came from a neighboring home on the other side of a vacant lot edged by small trees. Jim and his wife, Sue, didn't know the people living there and couldn't see what was happening. Nevertheless, the Patridges rushed toward the frantic cries. Sue arrived first. She shouted back, "Hurry, Jim. It's a baby!"

Jim found neighbor Tammy Kroll kneeling over the lifeless body of her one-year-old daughter, Jennifer. Moments before, Mrs. Kroll had found the toddler floating motionless in the family's backyard pool. She had attempted cardiopulmonary resuscitation without effect. Then she tried the telephone, dialing the operator for help. When she got a recorded message saying that operators were on strike, Mrs. Kroll began to scream, and the Patridges responded.

"The little girl was on a deck beside the pool," said Jim. "She wasn't breathing. She had no pulse. Her eyes were rolled back in her head, and she was blue all over, meaning she'd had no oxygen for a while. My wife got on the phone and called 911 for help, and I started first aid. In my heart, I felt certain the child was gone ... dead. But I hoped I could bring her back."

Jim initially performed the Heimlich maneuver on the baby, to clear any airway obstruction. Then he set about administering the CPR techniques he'd learned in a local hospital course he had taken, "just in case," a decade earlier. Breathe ... pump, pump, pump, pump, pump. Breathe ... pump, pump, pump, pump, pump. Breathe ....

Two minutes. Five minutes. Eight minutes. Ten minutes. No response to Jim's feverish efforts. "I kept checking and checking and couldn't get any pulse. It was frustrating. But I didn't want to let her go," he said. "I never considered that. I was going to stick with her, no matter what. I'd read some stories about where CPR had worked after a long time. I wanted her to have the same chance. Maybe if I kept oxygen moving, somebody could save her. I wasn't about to give up on her."

After about twelve minutes, Jim heard two things that sent a surge of hope through him. In the distance, there was the faint sound of a siren; help was approaching. In his ear, pressed against the baby's tiny chest, there was the first hint of a heartbeat, a thump ... th-thump. She was responding.

Then, in a sudden rush of activity, rescue workers were on the scene, taking charge, administering to the child, speeding her off to the hospital. She was released after a few days, with no ill effects at all.

"Hurry, Jim," his wife shouted. "It's a baby!"

The Krolls and the Patridges celebrated this news with shared gratitude and joy. The two families got to know each other, drew closer together, no longer lived side by side as strangers. To Jennifer, Jim became a godfather; to her family, he became a hero.

But to others who knew Jim, he had become a hero long before that fateful afternoon in West Chicago. There had been that day twenty years earlier when Private First Class Jim Patridge, an eighteen-year-old Marine Corps volunteer in the service of his country, had tripped the wire of a booby-trap while on a combat mission near Da Nang, South Vietnam. The resulting explosion took away both of his legs and most of his vision — but none of his heart.

He went through rehabilitation, learned to use a wheelchair, was fitted with artificial legs, then resumed his life. He got married and raised a family. On the day he heard Tammy Kroll scream, Jim had been the picture of domesticity, taking out the garbage!

"I was using my wheelchair at the time and didn't have my legs on," he explained. "Sue started running, and I followed in the chair, but it was slow going because the empty lot was bumpy, and about a hundred yards wide. I finally got across, but the trees blocked the chair completely, so I had to drop to the ground and swing myself on my arms the rest of the way — maybe twenty yards. That's when Sue hollered for me to hurry.

"When I pulled myself up onto the pool deck, Tammy Kroll didn't even notice my legs were missing. She said later that all she remembered was a man leaning over, bringing her baby back to life.

"I never came to terms with people calling me a hero. Couldn't get used to that," Jim Patridge said. "But there was one thing I felt real good about. After everything with saving Jennifer had died down, my teenaged son, Sean, put his arms around me, hugged me, and said, 'Dad, I'm proud of you.' He'd never done that before."

How many ways can heroism visit a man? That depends on how many people honor the worth of his deeds.

Greg Ysais with his wife, Andrea, daughter, Jessica, and family dog, Kimba.
(Photo © 1986 by Mike Kitada.)

Greg Ysais

Few people have ever actually looked into the jaws of death, willingly or otherwise. Greg Ysais of Mission Viejo, California, did so by choice, with a purpose: to rescue a dying child.

His horrifying experience descended on Greg in unlikely surroundings as he strolled with his wife, Andrea, and daughter, Jessica, through a nature preserve near famed San Juan Capistrano. The Ysaises were approaching the end of their walk when the solitude was broken by cries in the distance. Greg's family guessed that they were hearing children at play, but he suspected something more serious. He was right; they were hearing pleas for help.

Greg, a thirty-six-year-old instrumentation technician, realized that something was terribly wrong. He began jogging, then running, then sprinting through underbrush and small trees in the direction of the shrieks. Greg burst into a clearing and found a woman screaming hysterically and pointing. "A mountain lion!" she cried. "He grabbed my baby and carried her off!"

Dashing in the direction indicated by the distraught woman, Greg didn't know just what he was seeking or what he might find.

"I was looking for clues, signs, anything. I ran hard for a minute or so, through a lot of brush," he said. "Then I jumped over a bunch of cactus and came face-to-face with him."

Poised before Greg was a ferocious hundred-pound mountain lion, a breed of wild animal also known as a cougar or puma.

"The cat was back on his haunches with this little girl hanging from his jaws," said Greg. "His fangs were clamped down on her head and neck. She was moaning and squirming, but not really struggling.

"The cat was cornered, couldn't go anywhere. He was growling very low, as if to warn me off. Like a dog with a bone. He had his prey in his mouth, and he wasn't about to share it."

Greg remembered his only thought then was how he could separate the child from the animal without hurting the five-year-old girl any more than she already was.

He looked straight into the jaws of death.

"I ripped a good-sized branch from a tree stump and moved toward the cat," he said. "I got as close as I could — maybe four feet — and started yelling and swinging and jabbing at his head. I had to avoid the girl while distracting the animal so he would drop her. But he wouldn't. He kept growling, then started slashing, striking back at me with his right paw."

It became a duel for the life of the child who dangled like a rag doll from the cat's jaws: a primitive test of club versus claw.

"This went on for some time — a minute or two," Greg estimated. "The cat didn't want to give up, but little by little, he let her slip to the ground. I moved in swinging, and he backed off, yowling and clawing at me. When we'd gone a little way beyond the girl, I hollered back for her mom, who had followed me, to take her and run. The fight wasn't over, and I didn't know how things would go; I wanted the girl out of there. After a bit, the cat just quit. He sprang into the brush and darted away."

That was half the battle. Ahead lay the fight to keep life in the child, whose injuries were so horrible that her mother initially thought her dead. A spark of life remained, though, and Greg wanted to preserve it. Leaving the girl in her mother's care, he set off running toward a park gate to summon help. But his exertions had taken too much out of him; all but exhausted, Greg enlisted the aid of another man and got him to run on ahead.

The air soon was filled with the thunder of blades as a helicopter swooped in and whisked the pitifully mauled girl to a hospital. All that night and much of the next day, over twelve continuous hours, surgeons worked on her. In the end, although she lost one eye and suffered nerve damage, the child lived.

According to Greg, that was because of the doctors. "I didn't save her," he protested, "I only gave *them* a chance to."

Those modest words were characteristic of Greg Ysais, who was no less self-effacing than self-sacrificing. Having put someone else's life ahead of his own, he did the same with someone else's credit.

Kimberly Shingleton

Kim Shingleton sits on the cistern from which she rescued three-year-old Molly Geiling, who now sits securely on Kim's lap.
(Photo © by Janie Buntain, Lawrenceburg, Kentucky, The Anderson News.)

One word comes to mind at the mention of thirteen-year-old Kimberly Shingleton. The word is *courage*: unadorned, no-frills courage, simple and raw. It's the sort of courage that trips up your heartbeat and stands the hair at the back of your neck on end.

What brought her courage into full bloom was the intense heat of a crisis that is probably every farm family's nightmare: a child down a well. The child was Kim's cousin, Molly Geiling, just three years old; the well was the freshwater cistern behind Kim's home in rural Lawrenceburg, Kentucky.

The two girls had been playing hide-and-seek outdoors, and little Molly was "it." Evidently thinking that Kim might be hiding in the well, which was covered with a metal lid held in place by a large stone, Molly somehow managed to push the stone aside and lift the lid. Leaning over, peering into the dark depths of the well, she presumably lost her balance and tumbled in, unseen by anyone. Fortunately, her mother heard the metallic scrape of the lid moving and went to investigate. When she found no sign of Molly but saw the surface of the well water disturbed, she cried out.

For Kim's father, Earl, the first inkling of trouble was a shout from the back of the house: "Molly's in the well!"

"I found a flashlight, ran out, and looked down in there " said Earl. "The water was moving. Then Molly bobbed up to the surface, and you could see there was no life in her. She just rolled over and sank back under.

"I always kept a rope by the well, but it wasn't there. Later, I found that the kids had used it to put up a tire swing in the barn. But even if I'd had the rope, there wasn't much we could have done," he added. The opening to the well was only about a foot square — too small to admit any of the adults.

So Kimberly Shingleton volunteered to fill the breach.

"I said if Daddy and Mama held my feet and lowered me down into the well, maybe I could reach Molly," Kim explained in her soft Kentucky drawl. Minutes had already passed, and there was precious little time for pondering. Earl and DiAnna Shingleton grasped their young daughter by the ankles, turned her upside down, and eased her through the tiny portal into the well. There was a span of about eight feet from the opening to the water's surface.

"When I got down there, I was a foot or two short of the water," said Kim. "I hollered up that I couldn't reach. I said, 'Mama, I can't see Molly. I'm going to have to go in for her.' I told them to drop me, but they wouldn't. They started pulling me back up. So I kicked my feet to get loose. They hung on, but I kicked so hard they lost their grip." By her own choice, Kim Shingleton plunged headlong into the well.

Her parents were horrified. "I thought to myself, *Oh, God, now we're going to lose Kim, too*," said Earl. "It was horrible. We were running around up there and there wasn't nothing we could do. We were helpless." But their daughter was not.

"When I hit the water, all I felt was cold," related Kim. "It was the coldest I'd ever been. I wasn't thinking about the cold, though. I was thinking, *Where's Molly? I've got to find Molly*."

"Mama," she hollered, "I can't see Molly!"

She paddled her way around the entire surface of the well, which was about eight feet across, but found no trace of Molly. So what would Kim do, a schoolgirl all alone in the bitter-cold gloom with nothing to guide her and the lives of her cousin and herself hanging in the balance? She would search underwater.

"The first time I dove, I went down about ten feet. I didn't reach bottom," she said. "I had a hard time staying down. So I went up and caught my breath.

"I went all the way to the bottom the second time down. Daddy said it was maybe fifteen-feet deep. I searched all the corners, but still couldn't find her.

"The third time, I had my eyes open, and Mama was shining a light down. As I came back to the surface, I saw this little flash of color — purple. Now, Molly's got really long hair — it was in a braid — and I knew she had a purple ribbon in it that day. I grabbed for the color and saw the ribbon in my hand. I followed it down about six feet under the surface. I found Molly floating there, suspended. I dragged her up by the hair."

By now, Molly had been under the water for so long that it would claim her life if she didn't get help immediately.

"I pulled Molly over to the side and held on to a pipe with one hand," explained Kim. "With my other arm, I grabbed her around the middle and squeezed. You should have seen the water shoot out of her mouth! Then I patted her on the back, and she finally started coughing. After a little bit, she came around and was breathing on her own."

Earl, meantime, had located the missing rope, cut it down from the tire swing, and lowered it into the well. Kim tied it around Molly, who was lifted clear. Once wrapped in blankets and warmed up, Molly was none the worse for her ordeal.

"Me? I was almost frozen," said Kim. "When they pulled Molly up and I knew she was going to be okay, I realized that I couldn't feel my legs anymore. It's like I was in a bucket of ice, I was so cold. My hands were bad, too. I was numb. I couldn't get a grip on the rope. Daddy told me to put it around my leg and he would pull me up."

Kim's attitude toward the thrilling rescue of her cousin was almost matter-of-fact. "I wasn't afraid while I was down there, except I was scared I couldn't find Molly," she said. "I was happy that Molly was okay, and I was proud that I stayed calm."

But as her father observed, Kim had more to be proud of than calmness alone. "I think heroism is when you go beyond yourself," said Earl. "It's when you risk your own life to save the life of another person, which Kim did. I don't believe she gave any thought to herself or to her own safety. All she thought about was Molly. She put Molly's life before her own. And I think that's heroism."

Would anyone disagree?

HERITAGE & FAITH

Our reliance is in
the love of liberty which
God has planted in us.
Our defense is in the spirit
which prized liberty
as the heritage of all men,
in all lands everywhere.
Destroy this spirit
and you have planted
the seeds of despotism
at your own doors.

ABRAHAM LINCOLN
Speech, Edwardsville, Illinois
September 11, 1858

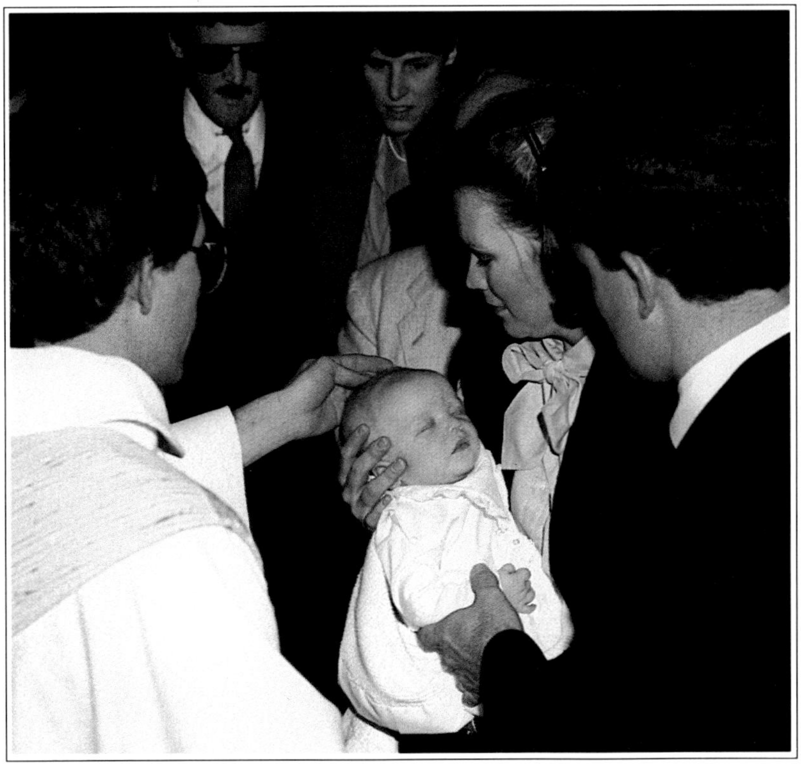

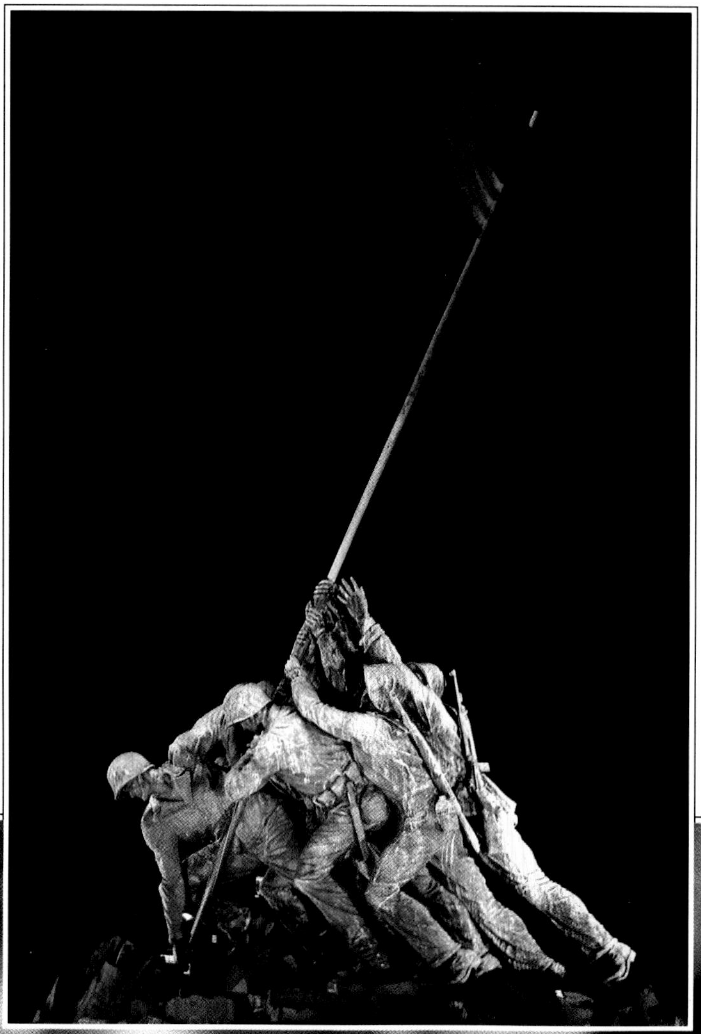

MARLBORO
So SUDBURY
BOSTON
Stow
MAYNARD
School

1776

A TRIBUTE TO MARK TWAIN

CHARITY

Charity wasn't invented by Americans, but with diligent practice they have made this gentle habit part of their national character.

Americans practice charity on a colossal scale, with vast agencies attending to domestic needs while the entire nation serves as an abundant reservoir for worldwide relief. This is the visible, public aspect of our charitable activities.

Distinct from that is the often unseen, private face of charity characterized by deeds of goodwill and benevolence carried out by individuals acting in the spirit of brotherly love. This spirit is crucial, for in the delicate balance of charity, the *how* of giving carries as much force as the *what*. Charity extended in a cold, desiccated, heartless manner; charity with a bitter, disagreeable taste about it; charity that degrades and humiliates — those are alien forms. Charity in the American spirit is sensitive, warm, compassionate. It is given with affection and humility and modesty. It is intended to aid the receiver, not aggrandize the giver. It is offered with the notion of bolstering the needy not only physically, but spiritually as well. It gives not so much a handout, as a hand up — with dignity and consideration. It sees poor people as people first and poor second.

The Bible says the poor are always with us; mercifully, so too are the charitable— among them, the countless Americans who practice charity as a way of life.

Dr. Francis J. Curry saying good-bye to one of his patients at St. Anthony's Medical Clinic.

Francis Curry

For Francis Curry, M.D., charity was a way of life from childhood on. As a boy he received it, and as a man he returned it, having learned in the getting of charity much about the giving of it.

"You know, I grew up poor in this very neighborhood of San Francisco," said Dr. Curry, indicating with a sweep of his arm the notorious Tenderloin section that surrounded him, an area of the city where people were drawn together by common bonds of poverty, need, and despair. "There were times as a boy that I had to accept charity, had to go for some free services. The people who provided those services said they were free, since you didn't pay any money for them. But I learned that they weren't free at all. You had to pay for them with a loss of your dignity by the way people at those charities humiliated you. It was like they were saying, 'Here we are, you lucky people: We're giving you something, we're doing you a big favor.' More than once, I found that the price was too high for me; I walked out rather than endure their indignities."

His dignity shaken but intact, Francis Curry never forgot the humiliation he felt at the hands of "charity." Though the experience he carried with him was negative, he was moved to do something positive about it if he got the opportunity.

"From the time I was eight until I was fifteen, I sold newspapers on the streets of the Tenderloin," he recalled. "I was a poor kid, one of those who didn't stand a chance of going anywhere. But I kept plugging and hoping that maybe something would break for me.

"Then one day a fellow pushed me to make an application for admission to college, which I did," said Dr. Curry, a gentle man so soft-spoken that his words sometimes bordered on whispers. "I got accepted. I had enough money to pay for one quarter's tuition, and I was so happy because I could go there and study for that one quarter and then be able to say that I had attended college.

"After a few weeks there, somebody — I don't know who — must have done something for me, since I found myself put on a scholarship. I figured they'd made a mistake of some kind, so I never took any breaks from school because I wanted to make as much progress as I could before they changed their minds. I attended summer terms and all, and never stopped for a rest."

In time, he earned a medical degree and began a distinguished academic and professional career, gaining recognition for his expertise in the treatment of tuberculosis and chest diseases, conducting a private practice, holding numerous medical school faculty appointments, and eventually becoming health director for the city and county of San Francisco.

In the rarified atmosphere at the top of society, Dr. Curry remained ever mindful of those at the bottom: the indigent, the neglected, the hopeless—the denizens of his old Tenderloin neighborhood.

He had frequently worked with impoverished people during his years as a practicing physician, but in 1958 he formalized his concern for the poor by opening a makeshift free chest clinic in the middle of the Tenderloin, situating it in a washroom beside the famous St. Anthony's Dining Room, where millions of free meals were served over the years.

"Lots of alcoholics from the streets went there, and I wanted to screen as many of them as I could for TB while they were on their way for a meal," he said.

Dr. Curry continued donating his services to the chest clinic over the next twenty years while keeping up his full range of professional and teaching activities and raising seven children. Then in 1976, the year of his nominal "retirement," he began a whole new career as founder, director, and chief practitioner at a full-service medical facility to replace the old chest clinic.

Called St. Anthony's Medical Clinic, it gave special meaning to the word *charity*.

"From the beginning, I said that our guiding philosophy—our motto and mission—in getting the clinic into operation would be the goal of working for the restoration of health, hope, and human dignity," he explained. "Of these, the most important was human dignity.

"It's like this," Dr. Curry went on. "If they didn't get medical treatment at the clinic, about 90 percent of the people we see wouldn't die. They would survive, but they would be sick and continue to be sick if they stayed away because they thought they would be humiliated at the clinic. On the other hand, by treating them with respect and encouraging them to come in, we can take care of their medical illnesses, do something to restore their dignity, and expect to see positive changes in many of the people we serve.

"One of the things I've found over the years is that you have to look beneath the surface of people. You have to look for good and expect to find it.

"For example, these skid row individuals are pretty rough on the outside but have a lot of good underneath," he said. "You'll see someone who's been sleeping in the streets and gutters. He comes in and he's dirty, he's filthy, he smells to high heaven. Maybe he's scratching all over and has lice.

"You talk with this person for a short while and you find that all of this surface stuff comes from the circumstances he's been forced to live in; this is all a product of his environment. When you get underneath all of this crusty stuff that's on the surface and you see the individual as a human being, you discover a fine and decent person.

"One fellow in particular comes to mind," Dr. Curry noted. "He used to show up at the clinic in pretty bad condition. But he was always friendly and considerate. When he would see me, he would call out, 'Wait just a minute, doctor.' Then he would carefully roll the sleeves of his coat and shirt way up and explain, 'I want to shake hands with you, but I don't want you to take any of my lice home to your lovely wife and children.' I would shake his hand and he would roll his sleeves back down.

"Now, this was a man whom most people referred to as a skid row bum. Yet he thought enough of me and my family that he wanted to take every precaution not to hurt us, even if those precautions embarrassed him. Where will you find that kind of concern on the part of charity clinic patients?"

You probably would find them in those clinics, like St. Anthony's, where that same brand of concern was practiced by the doctors and nurses. From his staff at St. Anthony's, Dr. Curry insisted on sensitivity and consideration toward all patients. Beyond the basic requirement of sound medical training, the first thing he looked for in his interviews with potential staff members was a caring attitude.

"I questioned applicants very closely," he said. "We would go over certain kinds of situations that might arise in the clinic, so I could find out whether they were able to work with me and learn to adopt my attitude that we were there for the patients, and not the other way around. I emphasized that we as physicians must treat our patients as we ourselves would like to be treated. I told them that the patient always comes first."

Over a period of eleven years, he built St. Anthony's into a facility with four paid nurses, twelve salaried physicians (though Dr. Curry himself received no compensation at all), and numerous volunteer medical interns and residents offering free care to all except obstetrics patients, who were referred to specialized institutions. Clinic doctors examined, treated, dispensed medicine to, did laboratory work on, and took X rays of about twenty thousand patients a year.

That the clinic survived without taking so much as a penny from its patients is one thing. Even more surprising was the fact that it never took a penny of tax support.

"I told the board of directors that I didn't want the bureaucratic red tape and wasted resources that go along with accepting government money," he remarked. "I said, 'If any tax money comes in, I quit.' So I guess they'll get along with private support and individual contributions as long as I'm here."

At the age of seventy-six, while still teaching and consulting at a local medical school and hospital, Dr. Curry continued supervising St. Anthony's Medical Clinic five days a week without pay.

"I owe a lot to life," he said by way of explaining his service. "I always felt that I should pay back my good fortune and share what I had, because there wouldn't have been any of this if somebody hadn't helped me along the way.

"It's like I always told my students: 'If you're hungry and somebody gives you a loaf of bread, even if you share the loaf with somebody else, you'll still have more than you had to begin with.' That's how charity works. Through the clinic, I'm sharing my loaf."

While he was never compensated for his long years of dedication to St. Anthony's, Dr. Curry did not go unrewarded, bittersweet though his rewards sometimes were.

"I got a phone call at home about two-thirty one morning," he said. "A skid row individual had been brought into the county hospital. He'd gotten drunk and was hit by a car. It didn't look good for him, and he wanted to talk to me. He pleaded with the people at the hospital. He told them, 'Call Dr. Curry and tell him I need to see him and it's important.' So finally they did. I got up and drove over to the hospital.

"Look for the good in people... and expect to find it."

"This injured man had been on the wagon, sober, for about fifteen years after having been an alcoholic for the longest time. I saw him originally at the old chest clinic. The thing that had beaten him down over the years, had driven him to skid row and to drink, was the fact that he had been falsely accused of a crime, convicted, and sent to San Quentin prison for something he always swore he didn't do. He could never get over that.

"Over the years, we worked with him, got him on the wagon, and talked about trying to arrange a pardon. It was our practice to involve ourselves in our patients' problems, and we knew that medical problems were not always the most serious ones.

"Well, that very day— the day of the night he was hit by the car — this man got word that he would receive a pardon from the governor, making him a first-class citizen again.

"So overjoyed was he that he went out to celebrate, started drinking for the first time in years, stepped into the street, and was struck by a car.

"He summoned me to the hospital to tell me he was sorry. He felt he'd disgraced me by getting drunk after we had gone to bat to help him get the pardon from the governor. 'I shouldn't have started drinking,' he told me. 'But I was so happy that I was a citizen and could vote again that I celebrated. I guess I let you down.'

"I told him that of course he hadn't let me down. I put my arms around him and held him. As I was holding him, he died. I'll always remember that this deathbed apology came from a charity patient."

That incident was sadder and more dramatic than most that Dr. Curry had experienced with his charity patients over the years, yet it was typical in what it said of his deeply affectionate relationship with all of them.

"Our word *charity* comes from the Latin root, *caritas*," Francis Curry explained. "The translation is simple. It means 'love.'"

Ruth Hardwick

Ruth Hardwick (foreground) at her Charity Restaurant in Perth Amboy, New Jersey. (Photo © William E. Sauro/The New York Times.)

Propped against a wall in a Perth Amboy, New Jersey, restaurant was a placard done up with fancy hand lettering that spelled out this inscription:

> And now abideth faith, hope, charity,
> these three;
> but the greatest of these is charity.
> *1 Corinthians 13:13*

Those few words from the Bible expressed the essence of this restaurant. Its meaning, its motivation, its mission was charity. And so was its name.

"Charity Restaurant was started to feed hungry people whether they can pay or not," explained its founder and guiding spirit, Ruth Hardwick. "We never say no to anyone. They can come in and eat — breakfast, lunch, dinner — and keep their dignity by donating whatever they can afford: a quarter, a dime, a nickel, nothing at all. We never ask questions. We tell them, 'Don't go hungry because you're proud but have no money. Charity Restaurant is for everyone and anyone.'

"We feed their bellies and their spirits, too," said Ruth, a seventy-year-old widow. "The poor, the sick, the people on drugs who come in here — we encourage them. We feed them, we pat them on the back, we touch them, we make contact with them. We show them that somebody loves them."

Mrs. Hardwick's own remarkable sense of love for people was illustrated by the circumstances that surrounded Charity Restaurant's opening. It was a happy occasion born of a profoundly sad event in Ruth's life.

"My daughter, Walterine, made a career of military service," Mrs. Hardwick said. "She was with the United States Army in West Germany. They told me that she died of heart failure. Went to sleep and never woke up. She was forty-four years old."

Ruth's husband had died only a couple of years earlier. Now, with the loss of her daughter as well, Mrs. Hardwick sank into deepest despair.

"I asked God time and again, 'Why Walterine? Why my daughter? Why would You take her and not me?'" the slight but energetic woman recollected. "I couldn't stop asking."

Presently, there came an answer that would turn Mrs. Hardwick's private pain into public relief.

The army informed her that Walterine had left a $50,000 life insurance policy with Ruth as the beneficiary. "When I heard that, I understood everything," she remarked. "I saw what I had to do."

Ruth had long believed that feeling sorry for needy people didn't mean much unless you also tried to do something for them. Yet she had been troubled by the unanswered question of what she, an elderly widow on a pension, could do to make any meaningful difference in the lives of the hungry — "people reaching their hands out for a crust of bread or surviving by eating dog food," she said.

This continuing puzzle was solved on the day she got word about her daughter's insurance policy. The tragedy that had closed one door in Ruth's life now opened another.

As a living memorial to Walterine, Mrs. Hardwick dedicated the insurance money and her own life to a single cause: feeding the hungry. Joining with a local church, she rented a Perth Amboy café that had gone out of business. Then she brought in food and supplies and began serving meals in the place she renamed Charity.

Ruth Hardwick welcomed all comers. Not just the derelicts and drifters from the streets, but also the elderly poor and the welfare families with children, people who usually had *something* to eat, but seldom had *enough*.

About twelve hundred people a week found their way to Charity Restaurant, where they were treated to the friendliness of Mrs. Hardwick's welcome as well as the nourishing goodness of the wholesome, home-cooked meals she supervised and sometimes prepared.

Tuesday through Sunday, she arose early in her Toms River, New Jersey, home so a volunteer could drive her the fifty miles to Perth Amboy in time to help fix and serve Charity's breakfast. At the end of the day, after the dinner dishes were cleared up and the tables were set for the next morning's breakfast, someone drove Ruth home again, making a round trip of a hundred miles daily.

"At the beginning, I worked twelve hours a day, seven days a week," she said. "But seven days got a little heavy for me at my stage of life. I thought, *If God rested one day, maybe I should, too.* So I started taking Mondays off."

But while Ruth could conserve her energy by taking an occasional day off, she couldn't do the same for her dwindling capital. It was true that most labor was volunteered and local businesses donated much of the food and supplies. Even so, the expense of rent, equipment, and utilities ate steadily into her

$50,000 and raised doubts about the restaurant's ability to survive. However, Ruth was determined to continue, and she did, for there was more in her heart than charity alone.

"You've got to have faith and hope," she said. "You've got to have positive thinking. I don't like that negative stuff. You need hope for the future and faith that God will provide things. We run Charity all with donations. Only donations that people give. We get wonderful donations — food, supplies, and some money, which we need more of.

"This restaurant is something I must do, can do, because I believe my daughter wanted it and I know that I do. I don't want this to die. I want it to continue when I'm gone. I'm giving my whole life to it.

"But like the book says, you can give everything but it has no meaning if you don't show charity," said Ruth Hardwick. "How can you say you love needy people and not show your love? I show it with charity." And, with Charity.

David Jones

David Jones with his wife, Jan, and daughter, Lindsey.

Charity as a way of life makes gentle human kindness a daily concern. For David Jones, it was a nightly concern, too.

On a particular night, David was asleep with his wife, Jan, and baby daughter, Lindsey, in their rural home near Holly Springs, North Carolina. It was 10:30 P.M., sooner than they usually retired, but they had gone to bed early because David, twenty-eight, had to take a difficult state insurance-sales licensing examination the next day.

As visions of test forms danced in his head, David was roused by the insistent blaring of a car horn outside his window. This sort of nocturnal intrusion was not unusual in those parts, he later explained. In the absence of street lighting, it could be dangerous for people to leave their cars and risk encountering snakes, vicious dogs, or other perils. So if a motorist needed something at night, he mostly just sat in his car outside a house and honked until someone turned on the lights and came out, as David Jones did.

He was greeted by the unexpected sight of an elderly woman in the company of a uniformed security guard from a nearby electric power plant.

"I found her in her car, stuck in a ditch back down the road," said the guard, nodding toward the woman. "She's out of gas and wants me to take her home, but I don't know this area because I'm not from around here. Could you see her home?"

This was not what David needed to hear. With so much riding on the next day's exam, he might reasonably have begged off with some plausible excuse. Or he might have grudgingly agreed, uttering an irritable, "Oh, all right!"

But that was not David's way.

"We're brought up to treat our neighbors as ourselves," he said, "and the Bible says we're to do this with love, with charity."

Flashing a smile at the old lady standing before him, David showed her into his home.

"She was shaky and scared and not in very good shape," he said of the woman who told him her name was "Miss Martha" and her age was eighty-two. "She was hungry, thirsty, tired, and seemed confused and disoriented. Jan and I thought that was from her ordeal of being stuck in the ditch.

"So we had her freshen up and take a shower while Jan cooked her some supper and I phoned our neighbors. He's our pastor, the Reverend David Ross. His wife, Susan, is a nurse," David Jones said.

"Susan examined Miss Martha and confirmed she was okay.

"But when Mr. Ross and I retrieved her car, we found that she'd burned up her power steering trying to get out of the ditch.

"It was real late by then," David went on, "and we invited Miss Martha to spend the night. She said fine. We suggested that she call her family and let them know that we'd drive her home in the morning."

When the bewildered older woman couldn't remember her phone number, the Joneses looked through her handbag and located a personal directory. To their amazement, it showed that she was from a different telephone area code. In fact, she lived so far away that her home was nearly in a different time zone!

The address in the book showed that she lived in Asheville, clear in the western tip of North Carolina, about 240 road miles away, and not very many miles short of the central time zone.

All of this just added to Miss Martha's befuddlement, because while she knew she had lost her way, she'd been convinced she was still in the vicinity of her home. Miss Martha told David that she'd left her home at nine o'clock that morning to buy shoes at a store a couple of miles away. Almost fourteen hours of aimless driving later, she showed up at David's door with no clear idea of how she'd gotten there.

"We called her family to assure them that Miss Martha was safe and in good hands," said David. "They were considerably relieved to hear that but angry, too, because this wasn't the first time she'd got herself lost.

"By that time, it was almost 3:00 A.M. We put Miss Martha to bed, telling her that we'd sort things out in the morning. Then we retired, too, and it was a short night because I had to be up and out the door by seven o'clock for my exam."

David dragged himself out of bed at dawn, managed to get through his insurance test, and returned home expecting that he would drive Miss Martha to the bus depot or airport for her trip to Asheville.

"We were simply living our faith"

"But she absolutely refused to go on a bus or plane by herself," he said. "Miss Martha said she was terrified to travel that way alone. She wanted to drive herself back home, but we obviously couldn't permit that, even if her car was up to it. We thought of having her relatives come from Asheville for her, but none of them could get away for several days."

David finally concluded that he must drive her home.

"It made for quite an eventful day after

getting three hours' sleep," he remarked as he told of the five-hour journey to Asheville.

"About every five minutes all the way there, Miss Martha would glimpse some landmark that seemed familiar to her and burst out with, 'Here's where I live!' or 'Oh, we're home now for sure!' or 'Are we there yet?' It was a long trip."

At last arriving in Asheville, David meant to deliver Miss Martha to her sister's home but drove her to her own home instead when she begged to be spared the embarrassing scolding she knew to expect from her family. He bid Miss Martha farewell, drove by her sister's home to let her know all was well, then motored the 240 miles back to Holly Springs.

It was well after midnight when David, having driven some five hundred miles that day, fell into bed. Lying there, he said, he felt pleased with the way things had worked out and gladdened that he and Jan and their neighbors, the Rosses, had experienced something not unlike the biblical parable of the Good Samaritan.

"We were simply living our faith," he said.

That was not quite the end of David's story, however, for there were two charming postscripts to report.

First, despite the distractions and fatigue occasioned by the previous night's events, David passed the state exam and qualified for his license.

Second, Miss Martha's family was so grateful to David for all he had done that they wished to give him a reward of two hundred dollars. "I protested and told them that I hadn't done it for money," he said. "But they pressed and were very insistent. To avoid hurting their feelings, I finally accepted it."

Then, quietly, David Jones gave it to charity.

John Fling

John Fling and a few of the children to whom he has become an everyday Santa Claus, with a truckload of gifts.

John Fling never gave anyone the shirt off his back.

He did give the socks off his feet (to a man who had no socks on a freezing winter's morning) and the raincoat off his shoulders (to a man without shelter in a downpour) and the watch off his wrist (to an elderly woman upset at always having to guess the time of day). In his personal approach to charity, he gave all of those plus decades of time and toil and much more.

"But I can't remember giving nobody my shirt," said John, insisting that shirt-off-the-back stories about him were exaggerated.

It was not easy to exaggerate the charitable exertions of John Fling — a man of sixty-six who by his own account had almost nothing material to show for a lifetime of hard work — because he had given away virtually everything he possessed to the needy.

"I don't have anything," he said. "I never have anything. Why, if I had five dollars at breakfast time, by lunch I'd be sure to meet somebody who needed it more than me, and I'd give it to them."

This sort of thing didn't happen because John was an easy touch, but because life was a hard task for many of his neighbors in Columbia, South Carolina. "The folks in misery," he called them: the old, the infirm, the lonely, the blind, the hungry, the children in need.

Even with a list that long, John did his best to look after people in misery for more than forty years in a selfless crusade that he laconically summed up by saying: "My whole life is helping people."

The good that John did, he achieved through personal sacrifice; he made life not quite so hard for others by making it not quite so easy for himself. Holding a regular job and living rent free in a place owned by his mother-in-law, he might well have accumulated all the trappings of material success. But in order to share what he had, John lived the simplest of lives.

"Me and Jane [his wife of forty-one years] don't go hungry, but we don't eat much, either. Cornbread and butter beans are enough for us. We don't have television. We don't take vacations. I haven't bought clothes, except underwear, in twenty years, and I collect and distribute donated clothes that are better than what I wear," he said, adding that he also didn't have a car, although he had owned and given away five of them over the years to families whose needs exceeded his own.

Besides the automobiles, John also managed to give away — in emergency rent payments, groceries, veterinary fees, and the like — much of what he earned from his job as a parts deliveryman for a Chevrolet dealer who cooperated with John by permitting him to set flexible work hours and mix charitable calls with his deliveries in a company truck.

Although he'd long since reached an age when many people sit back and take it easy, John remained tireless in his work for the needy.

"I never take a day off from helping people," he remarked. "I'm up at 5:30 A.M. and don't get back home at least till 9:30 P.M., seven days a week. It's sometimes later than that on weekends, because there's more to do then."

On one typical weekend, John set out at 7:00 A.M. Saturday with a bus load of blind people for an outing one hundred miles away. "I got home at one minute to midnight that night," he recalled.

"At five-thirty Sunday morning, I was up and out with the bus again, collecting several dozen children to attend my church. I haven't been to church by myself in thirty years; always got a bunch of kids with me. I live right next door to the church, but getting there and back takes me seven hours because of driving the young ones.

"As part of the Sunday routine," he said, "we always stop at a doughnut shop, since I know these children from the back streets of Columbia have had no breakfast. So it's doughnuts and drinks all round — about twenty-five dollars' worth. The church helps me with ten dollars, and the rest I come up with. After the doughnuts, it's back to the bus, never overloaded with weight, but always with happy noise.

"On the Saturday following that Sunday," John continued, "I took those same children and quite a few more — fifty-eight in all — to K mart at seven-thirty in the morning for a back-to-school shopping spree. This was their clothes for the year. K mart gave a good discount, but it still amounted to twenty-five or thirty dollars a child, some from donations that people gave and some from me. I felt blessed by the opportunity to help these kids."

As concerned as he was about the young in his community, John was perhaps even more concerned about and devoted to the blind, going out of his way on their account every day of every year.

"Blind folks are always needing something," he explained, "errands, repairs, supplies, transportation." Especially transportation. Over four decades, John estimated that he had put in forty thousand hours driving 400,000 miles to shuttle the blind to and from doctors' appointments, social service agencies, shopping trips, and recreational outings. When he wasn't taxiing them, he was taking care of them with a special affinity that he traced to a boyhood hunting accident that cost him the vision in his right eye. He placed particular emphasis on companionship for the blind, making sure they weren't forgotten, that they "didn't become hermits," as he put it.

Just about everything but the shirt off his back.

Despite all he did on behalf of the young and the blind, John still found time and energy enough to help the old, the disabled, and any others with special needs.

A dozen or more telephone calls came into his job or home every day, requesting help that he arranged as fast as he could get to it. Stopping between parts deliveries, he would change a light bulb for an elderly lady, fix a crippled man's wheelchair, buy a needy mother some baby formula (out of his own pocket), or clear an old man's plugged-up sink.

Regarded individually, none of these deeds might have seemed especially impressive. But viewed together, like the accumulation of minuscule tiles on a mosaic forty years in the making, they presented an overwhelming picture, the inspiration for which John explained with a simplicity that matched his unadorned life-style. "The Scriptures tell you to look after your neighbor," he said. "I always sleep better when I end the day knowing I'm helping people."

Asked how he'd gotten into helping the needy in the first place, John replied that he was born into it.

"I was the twelfth of nineteen children in a Georgia family so poor we weren't even sharecroppers," he remarked. "We were sharecroppers' helpers. But as poor as we were, somebody else was always poorer, always needing help.

"I got to thinking that the only way you get along in the world is by looking out for folks and sharing with the ones who've got less than you," John Fling said. "So I reckon if I came into the world with nothing, that's how I'll leave it." With nothing — except the love and affection of needy neighbors grateful for the enduring charity of a man who gave everything *but* the shirt off his back.

Bill Abbott

Bill Abbott and two helpers harvest a crop for the Food for the Needy program. (Photo by Chris Fitzgerald.)

"Charity means helping people to help themselves," Bill Abbott was saying. "It's the old story about the flour and the seed. Give a man a bag of flour, and he feeds his family for a week. Give him a bag of seed, and he feeds them for a lifetime."

A practical man by nature, Bill's philosophical turn of phrase reflected the temporary luxury of some free hours he was enjoying during a seasonal lull. It was the dead of winter, and his 170-acre Elmwood Farm in Hopkinton, Massachusetts, was frozen solid. With the spring planting still months away, Bill was taking the opportunity to reflect on his years of striving to feed the poor and help them feed themselves.

"Don't get me wrong," he remarked, "direct aid is fine. I've done a lot of it myself, and still do. But letting people take a hand in producing food for their own use is better. It has a more lasting effect than simply giving it to them. Self-help builds up self-esteem, so they appreciate the food more.

"When people from the housing projects in Boston have an opportunity to come out here and volunteer their labor on the farm," Bill continued, "they're working for *themselves*. They're going to take the fruits of their labor home to their tables."

Putting food on tables was something that Bill knew about from long experience. Over nearly two decades, hundreds of tons of vegetables from Elmwood Farm had found their way to the tables of thousands of poor people in Boston and Worcester, two large cities nearby. The food got there, free of charge, because Bill spent a great deal of his own money while working thirty hours a week, thirty weeks a year, tilling, weeding, and tending the ten acres of Elmwood land that he planted annually in high-yield vegetable crops.

"There were many places giving food to the poor," he said, "but hardly any of them provided fresh vegetables. You know: lettuce, tomatoes, peppers, cucumbers, squash, cabbages, and the like. So we got involved in that.

"My wife, Rose, and I originally started raising them when some clergymen came around and asked if we could help grow vegetables for feeding centers. We did that for a number of years, but then shifted away from giving to the centers in favor of sending our produce right to the poor in the housing projects."

When that change happened, Bill began offering the needy a chance to help themselves by working as volunteers in his "Food for the Needy" program. With the aid of a local church, he arranged free transportation so people could come from the cities to Bill's farm, where they worked at cultivating and harvesting the thirty to fifty tons of vegetables that he gave away each year.

After two bouts of heart-bypass surgery and almost twenty years of continuous sacrifice for the poor, Bill extended his commitment to those in need when he revealed tentative plans for selling off a large and valuable piece of Elmwood Farm in order to finance a charitable trust to provide still wider help.

"The idea would be to make low-interest loans available to hard-pressed farmers so they could increase their productivity by undertaking improvements they otherwise couldn't afford," he explained.

"In return, the loan agreement would stipulate that borrowers must donate their surplus crops to Food for the Needy, and maybe plant some crops expressly for the program as well.

"This is my way of doing something worthwhile with my stewardship of the land," Bill Abbott said. "I say stewardship because I've never felt that I owned this land, only that I was custodian of it. It was passed to me, and now I've had to decide how to pass it on. My choice is using it to help people help themselves. I couldn't think of anything better."

Nor could anyone else.

Rita Swiener is surrounded by some of her gifts for the needy.

Rita Swiener

The year is 1947.

The month is December.

The place is a Pittsburgh orphanage.

It is a bleak and lonesome institution, especially at holiday time, when most of the children have gone temporarily to the homes of relatives or other kindly people.

But a few kids have remained at the orphanage where a nice lady is giving out holiday presents to those left behind, one of whom — a little girl with large, dark eyes — is wriggling with anticipation.

Her gaze is riveted on a wondrous doll that closes its eyes when it lies down, then opens them again when it sits up. But now the girl spies something else among the prospective gifts — a nurse's kit, with bandages, medicines, and other intriguing stuff.

Which should she choose, the doll or the nurse's bag? She solves the quandary by gathering up both of them.

"No, child," the nice lady gently corrects her. "Don't you understand? You must choose one gift. Just one."

The youngster anxiously turns to her brother. But he's no help. He's busy picking out his own present. She turns back and looks from the doll to the kit, from the kit to the doll.

She longs to have both. And the two together would be so sensible! After all, she could use the kit to nurse the doll if it got sick.

Still, the little girl must make the painful choice, must take one and leave the other behind. Impulsively, she clutches at the doll, hugs it in a lingering embrace, then reluctantly puts it back and settles on the nurse's kit.

Fast forward forty years.

The orphan girl of the 1940s was now the career woman of the 1980s — successful, sophisticated, her passion for dolls and nurses' kits long forgotten. But not her passion for Christmas presents. They had been on the mind and in the heart of Rita Swiener for decades.

"My brother and I were adopted later, but I guess spending time in an orphanage where we were forced to choose just one gift left its mark on me," said Rita, a suburban St. Louis resident and professor of psychology at State Community College in East St. Louis. "I decided a long time ago I wanted to show needy kids that somebody cared at Christmas by making sure they got more than one gift."

An attractive single woman with a big smile and a store of energy to match, Rita Swiener said her Christmas work for poor children started while she was attending college in the 1960s. From modest beginnings there, involving a few gifts and a few hours around the holidays, her efforts grew into an impressive project demanding year-round dedication. "I have almost a thousand names on my Christmas list this year, and they'll all receive gifts," she said, explaining that she'd been given detailed information about people in need by Catholic Charities in St. Louis and several churches in East St. Louis. "Most are children, but their parents are also on the list, along with senior citizens and mental patients at two hospitals.

"The adults get one gift, but the kids all get more than one. Usually, if they're under the age of three, they receive two presents. Between three and five, they get three. And from age five on, five gifts go to each of them."

When someone suggested that this added up to a great number of presents, Rita agreed.

"Right now," she remarked one September, "I probably have over ten thousand individual gift items in my house: toys, games, sports equipment, gloves, mittens, mufflers, candy, cosmetics, little pieces of costume jewelry. All of them new. I start my shopping the day after Christmas, so I can get in on the postholiday clearances. During the rest of the year, I have three wholesale houses that let me have stuff cut-rate. I buy whatever I can in quantity, multiples of everything.

"I live by myself in a three-bedroom house with lots of closets," she went on. "One of those closets has my clothes in it. All the rest are filled with toys, gifts, wrapping paper, ribbon, and tape."

During most of her twenty-two-year campaign, Rita had paid for 100 percent of everything out of her own pocket. But in recent years, she said, public awareness of what she was doing had sparked donations toward wrapping paper, candy, and batteries for powered toys. Even so, she allowed that she was still picking up all but a tiny fraction of the cost — several thousand dollars a year.

Rita said it wasn't so much the gathering — but the distributing — of gifts that made the process so demanding, pointing out that the presents purchased by the thousands each year were not passed out randomly, but on a specific basis according to the names, addresses, and descriptions of need supplied to her by the churches and charities.

"I work steadily at buying and wrapping all through the year, but it still gets hectic at the end. Things really start rolling after Thanksgiving," she said. "Every one of the gifts will be individually wrapped and tagged with someone's name on it. I can't possibly do this alone. So after the school term lets out in early December, several of my students will volunteer to help. I also have a private patient who can't afford to pay for her treatment, so she pitches in and wraps toys instead.

"Just the same, I end up doing a majority of the work myself," said Rita. "From mid-December on, my place is turned into a Santa's workshop: twelve hours a day of nothing but wrapping, tying, writing and putting on tags, and sorting packages by neighborhoods and families for delivery.

A heart full of love, a house full of gifts.

"I have a troublesome arm that usually gives out under the strain, but the doctor keeps me going by prescribing anti-inflammatories. They usually get me through to the big day."

Actually, the big *days*, December 24 and 25.

With the aid of several auxiliary Santas whom she outfitted with full costumes (while she sported a "Santa's Helper" sweatshirt), Rita saw to it that the thousands of gifts were delivered by Santa "personally" in a carefully planned house-by-house, apartment-by-apartment blitz carried out in slightly more than twenty-four hours.

So exhausting did it become, Rita confessed, that she considered retiring on more than one occasion.

"I was ready to give it up just about every year," she said. "Every Christmas I'd say I can't go through this again. The house would be a disaster, and I'd be tired and fed up. But then as soon as we started giving out the presents, I'd be reminded of why I was doing it.

"It was the pure joy that I saw on those kids' faces when they'd get their gifts from Santa," Rita observed. "It was the greatest feeling in the world, seeing their eyes wide open, all lit up, and big smiles ear to ear." It was a vision that Rita witnessed often during each year's hectic drive to complete the deliveries.

"I generally started making the rounds at about one on Christmas Eve afternoon and would continue until two o'clock Christmas morning," she said. "I'd take a nap and start again at five in the morning on Christmas Day, and usually finish up at about three in the afternoon. By then I was exhausted and ready for a rest."

But, somebody pointed out, this left no time for Rita to observe her *own* Christmas.

"Oh, I never celebrate Christmas," she said. "I'm Jewish. A newspaper once called this the Jewish Santa project, but that was their idea, not mine. Religion's not my bag."

Rita's bag was Santa's bag.

"I love being Santa Claus," she said. "Being Santa means saying to a kid, 'Hey, the world cares about you.'

"I get to do this hundreds of times every Christmas, just by giving," said Rita, who fell silent for a moment, perhaps reliving the agony of an orphan girl compelled to make a heartbreaking choice. Then she added: "But never only one gift. Always more than one."

The men who line up to get food from Hattie Anthony's car.

Hattie Anthony

If giving when you can't afford it exemplifies charity on a memorable scale, who could ever forget Hattie Anthony?

Hattie was a middle-aged grandmother and foster parent of barely ordinary means but extraordinary charity, whose determination to give was sparked by an incident she saw one cold afternoon in Denver, where she lived. As Mrs. Anthony drove her dilapidated old car along Larimer Street in the city's skid row section, her disbelieving eyes were drawn to a sight that burned itself into her memory: A ragged street person hunched over, devouring scraps from a garbage can.

"He wasn't just poking and picking through the can," she emphasized. "He was *eating* out of it."

That vision shocked and repelled Hattie, who had known her own hard times when her family had gratefully accepted a charity food basket one holiday. But she had never known of anyone being brought to *this* — literally eating garbage.

At that moment, Mrs. Anthony resolved to put a stop to what she'd just seen, or at least to try. The question was, with what? Hattie, her husband, and two foster children hardly made ends meet; there was little money to spare. On the other hand, she was not without resources: She was a good cook and she had a good motive, "to feed the people that hunger," she said.

That night, Hattie lay awake trying to puzzle out this challenge. She thought and prayed, prayed and thought.

Presently, a plan took shape in her head.

The next morning she asked her husband, Howard, for a week's worth of the tips he collected from his shoe-shine job.

With that modest sum, she devoted several days to searching out bargains on plain but wholesome food — noodles, ground meat, pinto beans, cornmeal, and the like — which she set about preparing in her own kitchen. When it was cooked, Hattie loaded it into her car along with paper plates and plastic utensils. Then she drove to the very spot on Larimer Street where she had seen the man eating garbage. Exactly one week after witnessing that disturbing event, she served her first plate of food to Denver's street people.

"I go without so I can share with the people that hunger."

In the years that followed, she would serve tens of thousands more as her feeding plan blossomed into a small foundation that rented its own quarters, served hot meals on the street corner three times a week from the back of a donated van, and struggled along on donations from the community and unrelenting toil from Mrs. Anthony.

"I still do all the cooking myself, and we put out nine hundred meals a week sometimes," she noted shortly after the project had passed its fifth birthday. "I have a forty-one-quart pressure cooker, a big restaurant stove, and a lot of large pots and pans.

"My volunteer helper, Leo Woods, drives the van and sets things up when we serve on the street every Wednesday, Thursday, and Friday afternoon. But I dish everything onto the plates myself, and let me tell you, that's hard work. My back hurts a lot, and my feet, too, since I can't afford any good shoes," she went on. "Every time I save for a nice comfortable pair, I end up using the money for food, because I never turn anyone away.

"If you looked in the eyes of these people and saw them cold, bewildered, and neglected, you wouldn't turn them away, either.

"I've learned that even without money, you get along. You learn to pray. You learn to have faith. You learn to do without," she said. "I go without so I can share with the people that hunger."

Of selfless charity, those dozen words by Hattie Anthony spoke volumes. Unforgettably.

GENEROSITY

If there is any one trait that Americans have become renowned for and have built a well-earned reputation for the world over, it is their boundless generosity. At home and abroad, the prevailing (and accurate) image of the average American is not that of one who is mean and tightfisted, but one who is magnanimous and bighearted.

This American sense of generosity extends beyond shirt-off-the-back, my-meal-is-your-meal, material sharing, to encompass a readiness to share one's self as well. That is, generosity of deed and spirit: an open hand and an open heart. It is an attitude founded on both unselfishness and willingness: not only a disposition to share, but an active eagerness to share.

In its purest form, the generosity of Americans is always pursued in a spirit of genuine altruism. This means helping and sharing for their own sakes, without any thought of reward or recognition. Indeed, more than once I have heard modest people who were reluctant to discuss their generosity explain: "If you tell about it, it doesn't count."

Nevertheless, through persistent coaxing, several kindhearted Americans were convinced to tell about their generous ways. When you read their stories, you'll see that telling about generosity doesn't really make it count less; by the example set, it may even make it count more.

David Zullo

One memorably generous example was set by David Zullo of Baton Rouge, Louisiana. A twenty-eight-year-old paramedic, David's business was saving lives. Racing to disasters, he attended the injured and kept them alive with all of the technical equipment and know-how available to one in his profession.

But there was more to David than high-tech and training, first aid and fast trips to the hospital. He was a man of sensitivity and compassion, both on the job and off. And it was off the job — between emergency calls, actually — that David summoned up these qualities to "save" three lives in an unexpected way.

Behind the wheel of his ambulance one night, driving on an interstate that looped around Baton Rouge, David noticed two people trudging along dressed in dark clothes and carrying backpacks. The stretch of highway that they were approaching was particularly dangerous, without shoulders or lights. David knew that pedestrians there had to walk in the traffic lanes, where several people had been run down by motor vehicles in the past.

David didn't want to see that happen again; he decided to warn the pair. So he put on his flashing lights and stopped the ambulance beside them. Glancing out, he saw that they were a young man and woman, unwashed and unkempt.

What happened next wasn't revealed until many weeks later, when an unusual communication arrived at the editorial offices of the *Baton Rouge State Times*. It was a letter scrawled on a napkin that had been mailed to the newspaper inside an "envelope" fashioned from a Burger King hamburger bag. Misspellings and all, it was a message to the newspaper's editor from the couple David had stopped for on the road:

Dear Sir,
Somebody needs to know about what happens to us in your town. My husband and me is walking on the highway and been lost. We been hitching rides to Houston for work. This ambulance stops and they [the attendants] say get in.... He [the driver] said not to walk on the intrstate at nite or we get killed and I am pregnent with a baby....He asks if we are hungry and buys some Whoppers with his own money and with Cokes to drink....He drives us to the Travel Lodge and pays for a room and with his own money again. He is so nice I am crying. He dint treat us like Charity but he loves us and he dont even know us at all. He is like a story in the Bible. God says to feed the hungry and shelter the homeless. Thank you God for meeting David Zullo....

The newspaper investigated this story, learned the facts, and printed them, complete with the text of the woman's rough-hewn letter.

"When I read that, I cried," David admitted. "I hadn't known she was pregnant. She didn't say anything about it." Nor had David ever said much about his own actions, even though he had jeopardized his job and perhaps his life by stopping on the road to aid a couple of strangers. Why had he taken such risks?

"It was suicide walking out there. I could almost guarantee that these people were going to be killed. There was no way I could leave them," he said. "Besides, I figured it was better to pick them up in one piece then, than to go back after they'd been run down.

"I knew that I was risking the wrath of the department for breaking the rules if I stopped for them. But I had to do it, anyway, because this was a 'higher calling,' morally speaking. I had to make this choice."

When someone asked *why*, David explained that his choice that night was based on a choice he had made as a boy years before. On that earlier occasion, he had read about the lives of the saints and had been urged to choose one as his favorite, his patron saint.

"I chose Saint Martin," said David. "Martin was a fourth-century Roman army officer. A centurion, I think. Anyway, his men respected him so much that they gave him a beautiful cloak as a gift.

Beneath the dirt, he recognized dignity.

"One day he was marching at the head of his troops when he encountered a beggar on the road. The man had no clothes and was shivering from the cold. So Martin took his new cloak, cut it in two, and gave half to the beggar, thinking he recognized the features of Christ in the man."

David Zullo said from the moment he read that story, he wanted to be like Saint Martin and to help other people. That was why he became a paramedic, why he stopped on the highway outside Baton Rouge to help a pair of grimy travelers, and why he made a point of looking beyond their dirt to recognize their dignity.

Though they teetered on the ragged edge of existence, with no possessions but those in their knapsacks, they were determined to walk halfway across America to find a job. No panhandling, either, just hitching and hiking — reflecting their tenacious fight to maintain their self-respect, which was about all they had left. David took pains not to diminish it.

"You eat?" he inquired.

They said no, not in a day or so.

"Then how about joining me for a hamburger?"

The young couple allowed as how that would be just fine.

In a few minutes, they were downing their fill of burgers and soft drinks while David wondered aloud what their plans were for the cold night ahead. He suggested that they might put up at the Salvation Army or some other shelter.

They agreed that this would be a welcome prospect, except that a rule at most shelters prevented their sleeping together. Rather than be apart, they insisted, they would move on.

But David feared for their safety. "To keep them off the road that night," he said, "I was willing to do whatever it took."

What it took was a motel room that he told the couple he had "arranged" for.

"I lied a little," he confessed. "I said because I was a city official, I could set things up so that the city would pay for it as a public-safety kind of thing."

So David dropped them at the motel, wished them farewell, and returned to work after discretely paying their bill.

Back on the road, he felt relieved. Not only had he persuaded the two young people (who really were *three*) to accept the help they needed; he had done it in such a considerate way that they could take his generosity without giving up their self-respect. That was crucial, David knew; they would need it in the struggle ahead of them.

Fred Curling

If ever a word were suited to a man, the word *sharing* fit Fred Curling to a T.

"I didn't bring anything into the world, and I'm not going to take anything with me," observed the retired salesman from Chesapeake, Virginia. "What I have, I share."

That uncomplicated philosophy guided Fred for almost a decade as he brightened the lives of shut-ins by the hundreds at the Camelot Hall Nursing Home in Chesapeake.

Morning upon morning, month in and month out, 365 days a year, Fred appeared there promptly at 8:00 A.M., then spent the next four hours delivering flowers, cakes, and pies — along with his patented brand of cheerful smiles — to residents throughout the home.

Just as the smiles were beamed from Fred's heart and the flowers were gathered from his garden, so the cakes and pies he shared came from his own oven, which he switched on daily at 3:00 A.M., his regular waking time.

"I grew up on a farm," he chuckled by way of explaining his early rising. "I guess you can take the boy out of the country, but not the other way around."

"What I have,
I share."

For the people at Camelot Hall, Fred would spend several hours each morning at his baking, turning out occasional pies (coconut was his prize offering) but mostly cakes. He would cut these into serving-size pieces and wrap each individually. Then, after driving several miles from his house, he would distribute his treats throughout the nursing home where he began his daily sharing activities when his wife of more than fifty years was confined there in 1980.

She died several years later, but Fred went right on as before, ignoring the calendar and vowing to continue, despite the development of some medical problems in his eighty-fifth year.

"The people down there in the nursing home are old, and they need my help," he explained. "Many of them have very little, and quite a few have nothing at all. I don't have much myself, but what there is, I share. What I have is as free to those people as it is to me. It's as free as the air you breathe."

Igor Blonsky being congratulated by Police Chief Anthony Voelker on his promotion to detective. Left to right: son, Paul, daughter, Tamara, Chief Voelker, Igor, wife, Susan, Lt. James T. Cowan, Jr., and son, Michael.

Igor Blonsky

Material giving alone does not reveal the entire picture of generosity.

There's also an aspect of self-giving, a view of generosity favored by New York City policeman Igor Blonsky. "It means unselfishness," said the forty-three-year-old father of three teenagers. "It means helping others by giving of yourself."

On a dark, desolate night high above the Hudson River, Igor breathed life into his vision of generosity when he gave of himself, nearly gave *all* of himself, to help a troubled stranger.

It was 1:30 A.M. and Igor, an eighteen-year police veteran, was driving to his suburban home after a tour of duty in the Bronx. Starting across the Tappan Zee Bridge over the Hudson, he noticed a woman stop her car, get out, and walk to the rail.

"I was suspicious," Igor said. "I'd never seen a pedestrian on the bridge before. So I hit my brakes and backed up. As I got out of my car, I hollered, 'Hey! What's going on?'

"She looked at me with a blank kind of stare, then turned away and started climbing over the edge, fixing to jump," he said. "I vaulted over a railing onto a catwalk and lunged for her. She was one step from going over. I grabbed her arm. She struggled, and it flashed through my mind that I was going over with her. When I looked into that deep, dark nothingness down below, it scared the heck out of me. I got a surge of adrenaline and brought her under control.

"I helped her back inside the rail and said, 'Let's talk. My name is Igor, and I know you're going to think that's funny because everybody's always laughing at my name.' She never laughed. But I did manage to talk her into my car and back up about half a mile to the State Police barracks. Then they took over."

From the spot where Igor had stopped on the bridge, it was a drop of perhaps two hundred feet to the water, which he didn't see because of the darkness. So somebody asked him whether he ever went back for a daylight view.

"Are you kidding?" he responded. "It would never cross my mind to look over the edge of a bridge. If I look out a second-floor window, I get queasy. I'm terrified of heights!"

Every working day of his life, Igor was paid to face danger; jeopardy was part of his job. But why had he gone out of his way and involved himself in risky, frightening circumstances when he was off duty and homeward bound?

"The woman was out there alone, in the dark, in the middle of nowhere," he said. "Maybe there was an emergency. Who *knew* what was wrong? She looked desperate. She looked like she needed help."

And because Igor Blonsky cared enough to stop, that desperate need was met.

Brent Waguespack

There's not much to compare with a child's pure generosity. Its motivation is clear; its sincerity is evident.

Hallmarked by purity at every turn was the guileless generosity of ten-year-old Brent Waguespack, a Shreveport, Louisiana, boy described by his mother as a kindhearted child, but no angel or do-gooder.

"He's just a frogs-in-the-pocket, ordinary kid," said Deborah Waguespack, whose son taught her that an ordinary kid, when suitably motivated, is capable of extraordinary tenderness and concern.

Brent and his folks had recently moved to Shreveport from Baton Rouge, where they maintained close family ties. Baton Rouge newspapers arrived regularly at their house, and it was in one of these that Brent came across a sad story, complete with photographs, about the child-abuse death of a three-year-old boy whose family could not afford a funeral.

Deborah recalled that Brent seemed troubled by the report and went so far as to bring it to her attention. "Did you see this, Mom?" he asked in a perplexed tone. "Just look at this poor little boy." Brent then cut out the story and set it aside.

Why he did that, Deborah learned some days later, when relatives phoned from Baton Rouge to say that a local newspaper, the *Advocate*, had run a story telling of a heartwarming letter Brent wrote to the hospital where the abused child had died.

"Dear hospital here's my donation to the little boy that died. Its not a lot, but it's all I could do," said Brent's letter, which had $1.30 enclosed with it. The youngster went on to note that he was only ten years old, and said: "The picture in the newspaper made me cry. I'm just a boy but boys have fellings to."

Brent had written the letter and sent his contribution toward the battered child's funeral entirely on his own, without the urging or knowledge of anyone else. The world would never have known about it if the hospital hadn't shared his letter with the newspaper.

Brent's donation of $1.30 was in nickels and dimes. His mother speculated that since he didn't receive an allowance and had no other resources, he had probably saved it from his lunch money over a number of days — a sacrifice that touched many people.

"Letters and calls came from everywhere, praising Brent's generosity and telling him it was okay for a boy to have feelings," said Mrs. Waguespack. "All the fuss puzzled Brent. He couldn't understand people's interest. He told me, 'I was only trying to be kind.'"

Denise McClain and Carolyn Carideo.

Denise McClain

One measure of people's generosity is the level of sacrifice they're prepared to make in the interest of others. Many are ready to give when it's easy, some when it's difficult, a few when it's painfully hard.

Among those few was twenty-three-year-old Denise McClain.

A registered nurse at a hospital in Erie, Pennsylvania, Denise was on duty late one night when a patient call-light began blinking at her station on a medical-surgical floor. She started to respond but took only a few steps down the hall before she grasped what was wrong: Smoke was billowing out of the room from which the call signal was coming.

"Fire is absolutely the worst thing that can happen in a hospital filled with helpless patients. It's a killer," she said. "So I pulled the fire alarm, which is what you're always supposed to do first, and then ran to the room."

A horrifying sight met her eyes. Flames and heavy smoke were rising from the bed of an elderly patient who had been restrained with a device that the nurses called a "posey." The cloth-strip restraint was tied to one of the man's wrists and to a side rail of the bed to keep him from falling out and being injured.

"This old man was squirming, trying to get away from the fire that was all around him," Denise remembered. "The mattress, the draw curtain that encloses the bed, even the floor tiles were burning. But as bad as the fire was, the smoke was ten times as bad — the worst I ever saw."

Joined by licensed practical nurse Carolyn Carideo, Denise rushed into the room and set off a second alarm by yanking the call-bell cord out of the wall. Then the two women tried to lift the patient from the bed. They couldn't, however, because of the restraining device: It would have to be unfastened to save him. But to their dismay, the posey itself was on fire. So they attempted to snap it by yanking at the parts that were not burning. They failed.

By now, the clock was running out for both patient and nurses. If the flames didn't get them, the thick, deadly smoke would.

"It got scary when conditions turned so bad," said Denise. "At one point I was afraid none of us would make it. Personally, I realized I had to set the man free, or else. He was a patient, and I couldn't leave him. I knew that if *I* wanted to survive, I'd have to make sure *he* survived."

At this point, Denise McClain made a do-or-die decision that was as remarkable for its gutsiness as for its self-sacrifice: She thrust her hands directly into the flames and tried to untie the burning posey that held the man in its fiery grip.

"I knew my hands would burn, so I tried not to think about it. I concentrated on getting him untied, because I saw if I didn't, he would die," Denise recounted. "It was no good, though. I tried several times but realized I wasn't going to get it undone."

Denise withdrew her hands from the fire and hollered for other nurses who had come running to find her something she could use to cut the bindings.

"I could scarcely breathe anymore because of the smoke," she said. "It was so thick that I could hardly see when somebody passed a pair of shears into the room." However, she saw well enough to make out the burning posey; she plunged her hands into the flames again.

This time, she succeeded. Quickly slashing through the restraint, she assisted the man out of bed and guided him around the burning tiles to safety. Then, as the flames were being extinguished, Denise and other nurses rushed through the halls, closing and sealing doors to keep the smoke from reaching other patients.

It was only after calm was restored that Denise began to realize the consequences of her actions. Although she succeeded in keeping the patient's burns to a minimum, Denise herself was severely and painfully injured. She suffered second- and third-degree burns to her right hand and first-degree burns to her arms and face. In addition, her hair was singed, her teeth were blackened, and she was treated for smoke inhalation.

She gave
when it really hurt.

"I was in the hospital for four days," she said, "and then I went through burn rehabilitation for a month. I was off work for about five weeks."

Insisting that "you have to sort of put yourself in second place" in situations like these, Denise McClain dismissed the sacrifice as a measure of her responsibility. But in truth it was a measure of her generosity: her readiness to give when it hurt.

The Ripleys

Many generous people would readily share their possessions with individuals in need. Some would share their food. Some might even share their homes. Merrily and Ted Ripley shared all of these things and more; they shared their lives.

Starting in 1969, when they had three children of their own living at home in Port Angeles, Washington, the Ripleys began enlarging their family through adoption. They added youngsters mostly by ones and twos, but once took on five siblings from Guatemala. The Ripley house on Black Diamond Road became home to kids of many shades, hues, races, nationalities, and languages.

By the time their family was completed, Ted and Merrily had twenty-two children in all: three biological, eighteen adopted, one foster child.

The Ripleys bore all of the expense with no outside help, which required plenty of material sacrifice to accommodate such a throng: food and supplies bought by the gross, the bushel, the hundredweight; a new washing machine every year.

It took a lot of logistical planning, too. For example, the Ripleys almost never went anywhere all at the same time. Even then, it could be confusing. Once when Merrily and Ted arrived at a picnic ground with a dozen kids in tow, someone asked whether they were a church group, touching off the following exchange:

"No, we're just one family."

"You mean these are *all* your children?"

"Oh, not *all* of our children. We left ten at home!"

Despite their struggles and tribulations, the Ripleys had no regrets. "Sure, we're looking forward to emptying the nest," said Merrily. "But our personal rewards have been tremendous, worth whatever we gave up along the way."

"This was something we wanted to do," added Ted, a trial lawyer by profession. "It was a matter of choice, of priorities, of how we wanted to use our resources and live our life.

"The commitment we felt was reinforced every time we saw a positive response or a new achievement from a child —a kid who might otherwise have had no opportunity, but now did. Then we knew we were helping, making their lives better and more complete. Ours, too."

David Munch

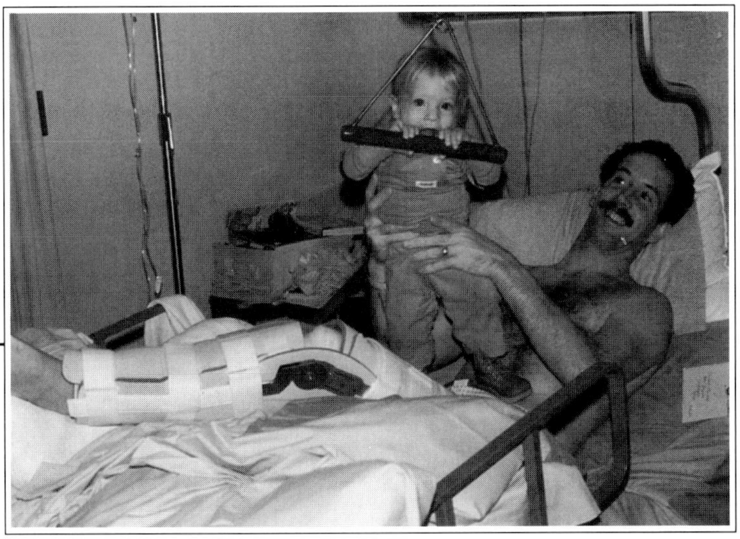

Dr. David Munch with his son, Ryan.

The reasons for Dr. David Munch of Englewood, Colorado, *not* to stop at a late-night highway crash were many. He could have told himself: *It might endanger my wife and baby sleeping next to me. It might be risky for me. It might hurt my new medical practice. I might get sued. I don't know what's going on. It's not my job.* With justification, he might have cited any of these or many other excuses for passing by.

Instead, he stopped, for just one reason. "I thought I could help," he would say later in recalling what happened on Denver's Sixth Avenue Freeway one cold February night.

The high price of generosity– paid in full.

"My wife, Joan, our son, Ryan, and I were driving home about midnight when we came upon an accident just after it happened," said David, thirty, an internist who only a few months earlier had begun his medical practice in suburban Aurora. "Two cars had collided, and one was overturned, resting on its roof on the right shoulder of the road. A young couple were belted in their seats, hanging upside down. But their baby had come out of his infant chair and landed on the roof, which was now the car's floor.

"During my hospital residency days, I'd seen a number of injuries that had occurred not *during* accidents, but *after*, when people who meant well but didn't know how to handle these situations had gotten involved," David pointed out. "And with a rollover accident like this, the potential danger was especially great because of the likelihood of head and neck injuries. I wanted to be on the scene to make sure that rescuers didn't add to the victims' injuries."

David got out of his car, asked some bystanders to control passing traffic, and approached the wrecked automobile.

"I could see the parents were okay, and I could hear the baby crying, which was a good sign because it meant he was conscious.

"A window was open. I crawled in and immobilized the infant's head and neck by supporting it with my hand and arm to prevent any spinal-cord damage. As I got out, I noticed that the baby was wearing only light clothes. It was cold out, so I walked over to ask some ladies for a blanket," David recounted.

"Then somebody hollered, 'Look out! Look out!' and I heard a screech of tires."

David had no recollection of what followed, which was probably just as well, because a third car veered into the crash site and hit the young physician from behind, hard. David went in one direction; the baby he'd been holding went in another.

Landing at the feet of David's wife, the two-month-old boy was found to have a head injury, but he was released from the hospital after a couple of days with no permanent damage. David, however, was not so fortunate.

"Somebody told me later that I came up and bounced off the hood of the car that hit me, then smacked my head off the windshield and sailed some distance. I hit another person and actually broke his arm as I flew through the air. I finally landed on the pavement. This was all described to me after the fact. I don't remember any of it," he said.

"When I woke up on the freeway, I started checking myself out: head, okay; neck, okay; chest, okay; abdomen, okay. But when I got to my legs, I knew I was in trouble," Dr. Munch related. "My right knee and the back of my left leg were mangled, crushed. The left leg lost a lot of muscle that never came back, and most of the cartilage had to be removed from the right knee. I spent three months in the hospital, underwent four different operations. When I finally resumed my medical practice, I was on crutches with both legs in casts."

The casts eventually came off, but David was never quite the same. Before that night on the freeway, he had been an avid amateur athlete, a bicyclist, swimmer, and long-distance runner used to participating in big local races. But the accident ended his running, just as it might have ended his career or his life.

Nevertheless, David's generous instincts were not dulled. "If I had to," he said while still undergoing rehabilitation, "even knowing the consequences, I would do the same again." From some people, that might have been just so much talk. Not David Munch. He backed up his words with actions.

While driving to his office one morning a couple of years later, he again came upon a traffic accident. Again, he stopped.

"This time, a boy of ten or twelve had been hit by a car and knocked off his bike on a busy road," he said. "Just as before, nobody on hand knew what to do and I was concerned about their compounding the boy's injuries. So I took charge, although this time I devoted more attention to traffic control first. I assigned specific people to stop and hold traffic before I tended to the boy. We were right in the middle of a traffic lane. It was eerie ... *déjà vu* ... experience repeating itself. I could feel the hair rising on my neck. But everything worked just fine, and it turned out the boy was not badly hurt. That made me glad."

Even knowing the toll that could be exacted, David had been prepared to pay the price of generosity a second time. He explained that it was a matter of principle. "The principle here," he said, "was helping. The prospect of helping a suffering person, or even saving a life."

Circumstances may change, but principles don't. With the right principles, David Munch did the right thing — twice.

Paul Rogers being congratulated by Major General Thomas G. Darling, U.S.A.F.

Paul Rogers

Today's fitness-conscious America puts a premium on athletic prowess, making superior performance a source of pride for millions of competitors.

In this respect, sixteen-year-old Paul Rogers of Norfolk, Virginia, was no different from most of the several thousand contestants who were running one Saturday in Norfolk's biggest footrace of the year. He had trained hard for the event and harbored proud hopes of setting a personal record.

Even so, when a stranger needed help, Paul readily sacrificed his pride.

The high school junior was about halfway through the 6.2-mile race, well up in the field of runners, on a pace that might have brought him a personal best, when the man directly in front of him seemed to stumble. Then he staggered and fell.

In situations like these, some zealous competitors might have taken an "every man for himself" approach: veer to the left, swerve to the right, jump over, but never stop for a fallen opponent. After all, the time sacrificed could mean a trophy lost or a record missed. But this attitude was not to Paul Rogers' liking.

In the long run, a champion.

"I stopped to help him up," said Paul. "I thought the guy had tripped. But when I looked closer, I knew he was in trouble; he was having a heart attack. He was breathing when I reached him, then everything stopped—heart, lungs—the works. He was in cardiac arrest. So I began administering CPR, which I had learned from my dad. After a bit, a nurse who was running stopped and helped me, and the paramedics arrived a few minutes later." Their combined efforts notwithstanding, the man died.

And Paul never completed the race. Yet on a day when he failed even to cross the finish line, Paul Rogers proved himself a champion where it counted.

Mr. and Mrs. Lou Stouffer.

Lou is Santa Claus.

The Stouffers

It was almost Christmas in the mountain country of Preston County, West Virginia, but at one isolated home the only seasonal signs were the signs of winter: cold and dark. There was an atmosphere not of festivity but poverty; the house was without heat, electricity, or plumbing. Gathered in its otherwise empty parlor were seven barefoot children whose clothes were as spotless as they were threadbare. The youngsters themselves had been scrubbed to within an inch of their lives. Suddenly, there was a commotion at the front door. In the parlor, the mood changed; the gloom dissipated. The children's eyes first widened, then crinkled at the edges as timid smiles spread across their faces in response to a jolly, older man who entered the room. Flowing white hair fell over his fur collar, and his long white beard reached to the middle of his chest. He was clad all in red, as was the woman beside him. Lou and Lola Stouffer were making another Christmas call.

Every December for more than fifteen years, Lou and Lola played out a kind of rural *Miracle on 34th Street*, fulfilling the holiday dreams of needy families and following up on the Santa Claus mail that the local post office routinely forwarded not to the North Pole but to the Stouffer home in Terra Alta, West Virginia.

Originally in a station wagon that they virtually drove into the ground, and later in a four-wheel-drive truck that someone gave to them, each holiday season the Stouffers traveled more than five thousand miles over treacherous, unpaved mountain roads to visit five hundred or so families in Preston County and neighboring Garrett County, Maryland. That was an area of the Appalachians that mining and railroading had passed by, leaving in their wake unemployment and want.

Unable to do anything about jobs, the Stouffers concentrated on relieving the want — something they themselves had known in their lives. "We've both felt what it's like to do without, but we were raised believing that to give is better than to get," said Lola. "God wants us to share what we have. You ask anyone around here and they'll tell you Lou would give them the shirt off his back. And I remember sending my children off to Sunday school a lot of times with only a penny for the collection plate because that's all we had. But even if it was just a penny, we shared it, and that felt good."

"Even if it was just a penny, we shared it — and that felt good."

By the time they had reached their sixties and were blessed with many grandchildren, circumstances had improved for the Stouffers. Lou, whose striking white beard covered his face all year long, ran an auto-body shop; Lola worked at the local high school. Although they then had more than pennies to share, their ongoing generosity represented real sacrifice.

They spent twelve months a year buying or receiving donations of new and used toys and clothes. They refurbished every used toy and made sure that each piece of clothing was clean and in good repair. They stockpiled their bounty throughout the year and then boxed it according to the individual needs of each family. Whenever possible, they included food in the box. Then in the weeks leading up to Christmas, they would spend as much as eighteen hours a day driving to remote points for their deliveries, usually finishing between 3:00 and 4:00 A.M. Christmas morning.

Finally, they would attend early church services and return home to celebrate the holiday, but not with the usual exchange of gifts. "We never give each other Christmas presents," explained Lola, "because whatever we would spend on ourselves, we spend instead on the needy children. Their happy faces and the tears we sometimes see in their parents' eyes — those are our gifts. They make us feel real young, so I guess we should keep going for quite a while."

After many years of anonymous toil, there came an occasion one December for Lou and Lola to be recognized for what they were — two loving, caring, generous people. A network television morning program invited the Stouffers to appear as guests on the show. But "Mr. and Mrs. Santa" of the Appalachian Mountains politely declined. "No time. Too many children depending on us," said Lou. "We do this for the kids, not the fame."

AMERICAN FACES

**In thy face I see
The map of honor, truth,
and loyalty.**

WILLIAM SHAKESPEARE
Henry VI, Part II

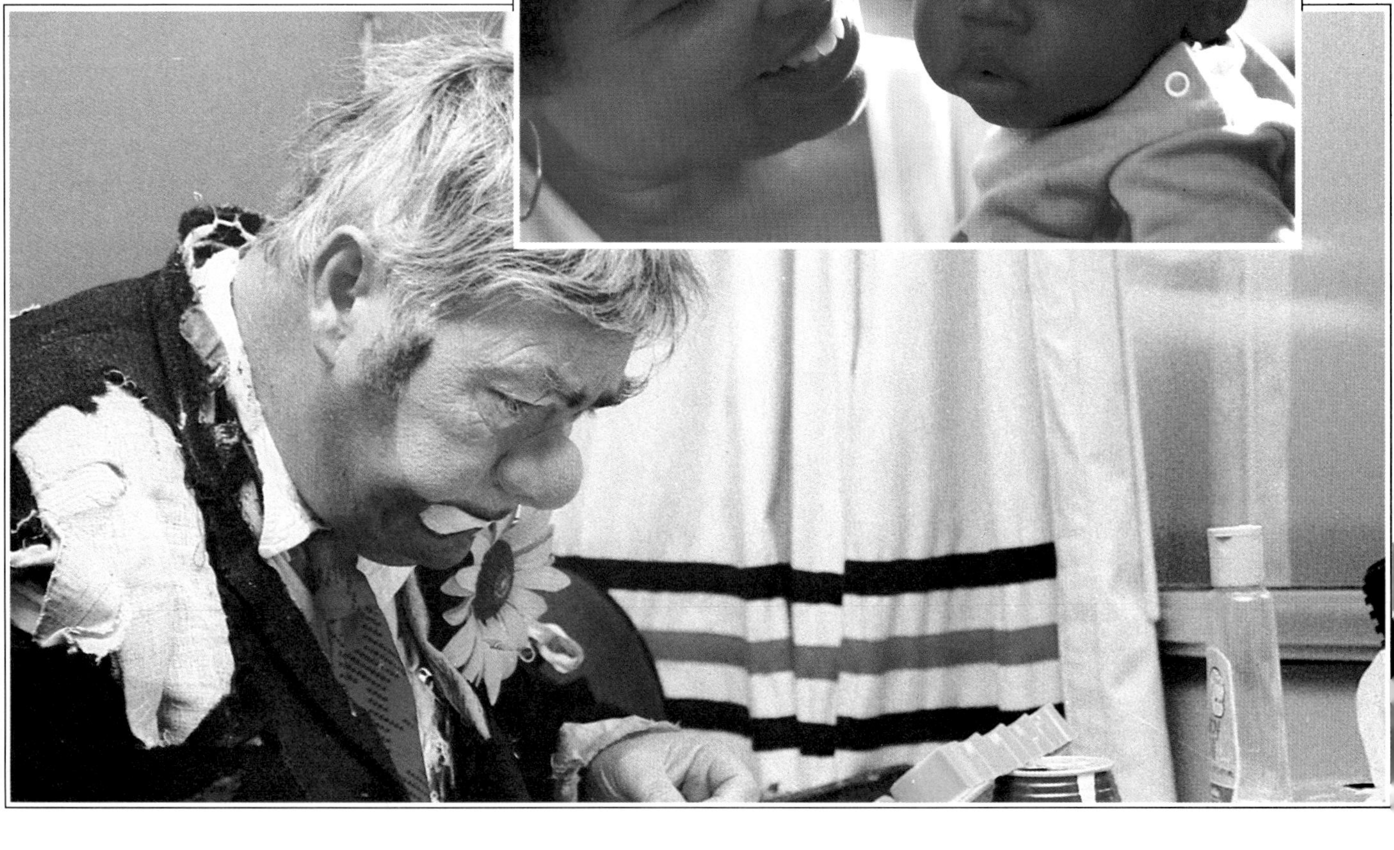

GAHILL
H.A.B.

HISTORICAL
BURR-ARCH
GUILFORD
JALAPENO SAM

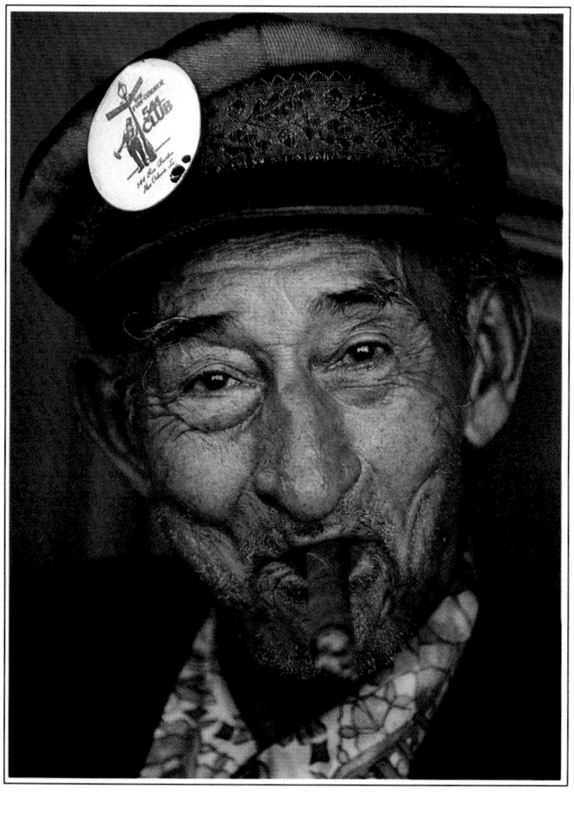
THE FUN CORNER
CLUB

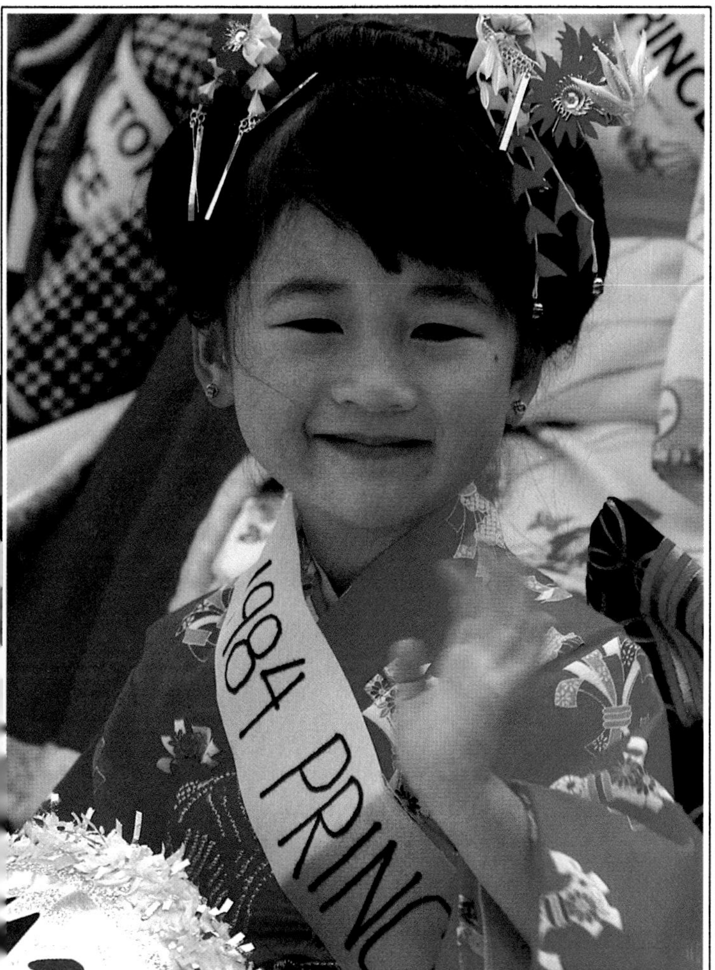
1984 PRINC

HONESTY

Americans prize honesty, for honesty is the backbone of our character. No personal or national trait is more highly revered than this simplest one of all. We respect it and expect it in ourselves, our associates, our leaders.

There is no better honor or compliment that we can pay than to call someone "honest." How, for example, do we remember one of the greatest of our presidents? Not as compassionate, courageous, brilliant, wise, crafty, artful, or humorous, even though he was all of those things. No, we remember him as "Honest Abe" Lincoln. It is an oversimplification to reduce a man's life to a single descriptive word. Yet that was the tribute paid to Lincoln in his own lifetime, and that is how he has remained in our national consciousness. With fondness and reverence, *honest* is the word we use to sum up his multidimensional life.

And why not? Honesty itself is multidimensional, suggesting more than trustworthiness in a material sense. It implies as well integrity, ethicality, truthfulness, straight shooting, square dealing, decency — in an active and purposeful way. Honest people act as they do, not because dishonesty is *wrong* but because honesty is *right*. Honesty, then, is a positive disposition.

We may hear and see sensational accounts of mendacious, duplicitous, corrupt politicians and double-dealing, unscrupulous business operators. These, however, are the exception. The rule is honesty. Because long after the crooks and cheats have faded from our memories, we will recall the pervasiveness of principle. We will remember the people who showed integrity when it wasn't convenient, who did the right thing when it would have been easier (and perhaps more profitable) to do the wrong, who were honest when they didn't *have* to be.

Earl and Mary Wilson found more than litter on their Tuesday morning hunt for bottles and cans. (Photo © Des Moines Register/David Peterson.)

Earl and Mary Wilson

Earl and Mary Wilson, of Des Moines, Iowa, need not have acted honestly. No one would ever have been the wiser had the Wilsons pocketed the bagful of cash they found in a parking lot.

"But that's not our way of doing things. We've lived our life honest and figure on keeping it that way," said Earl, as he talked about why he and his wife never kept the money-filled bag they discovered early one morning.

It was about 6:00 A.M. As usual, the Wilsons — Earl, eighty, and his wife, seventy-nine — had been up since 4:30. They arose at that hour to get a head start on their regular routine of searching roadsides and dumpsters for returnable beverage cans and bottles that brought in two or three dollars a day to supplement Earl's Social Security check, their only other source of income.

A clear conscience because, "We did it our way."

On this particular day, the couple, married fifty-five years, were making their way across a parking lot behind a Des Moines cocktail lounge when they all but stumbled over the bank bag that lay in plain view.

They peeked inside and saw cash, lots of cash, which could have come in handy for the Wilsons, who faced unusual medical expenses because of recent eye surgery Mary had undergone. Along with the money, at the bottom of the container, was a small pistol. Earl and Mary wanted no part of anything in the bag.

"We're too old to start keeping other people's property," remarked Earl. "We never touched it or counted it or nothing. We just took it down to the police."

Officers who examined the bag before returning it to a local business from which it had disappeared several days earlier totaled up more than eight hundred dollars in small bills. That amount was the equivalent of some sixteen thousand returnable cans and bottles at a nickel apiece, or about a year's worth of collecting for the Wilsons.

"Some folks told us we could have throwed away the bag and kept the money," said Earl. "But we did it our way. So our conscience was clear and we didn't have nothing to worry about. We felt good."

Earl and Mary Wilson never got a reward for what they did, so financially were no richer than before. But spiritually, they came away far richer.

William Scholtz (left) who received a premium on his silver coins from Cudahy Bank president, Hal Knuth, and employee Eileen Dusenbery.

Cudahy Bank

There's more to honesty than the absence of larceny; there's also the presence of decency.

This active feature of honesty was explored in a heartwarming turn of events at the First National Bank of Cudahy, Wisconsin. Eileen Dusenbery was at her teller's post one day when an elderly man in an obvious state of agitation approached and asked her to convert about five hundred old-fashioned silver half-dollars into currency. Eileen gently suggested that the coins might be worth more than their face value, but the man insisted that he needed the money immediately, so she complied.

When he had gone, however, she related the matter to bank president Hal Knuth, who examined the coins and said that they did indeed have greater value than the $251.50 Eileen had given the man. Setting the coins aside, Hal told her and the rest of the staff to keep an eye out and alert him if the man returned to the bank.

About a week and a half later, a staff member spotted the old man at a drive-in window and told Hal, who sent to have him brought in. Sitting him down, the bank president informed the man that he had been hasty in disposing of the coins, which were quite valuable. On hearing this, the customer broke down and began to cry. He explained through his sobs that he and his wife had saved the half-dollars during forty years of marriage, and that he had rushed to turn them and anything else of value in their home into cash so that he could cover the expense of his wife's cancer treatments.

"Don't you worry," Hal assured the man, squeezing his shoulder. "We held onto the coins. If you'll give us permission, we'll get them appraised to find out what they're really worth." The man readily consented, and a few days later, Hal gave him a check for more than $6,500 over and above the face value of the coins. When the old man showed the check to his wife, she managed a smile — her first in a long time. Sadly, it was also one of her last. She died shortly afterward.

Still, the incident with the coins had put some cheer into the couple's final days together, while relieving them of at least one burden. And Hal Knuth said it was a wonderful experience for the bank, his staff, their customers, the business community, and the community at large.

"When word of what happened got around, we received letters from everywhere — bushels and bushels of mail," Hal recalled. "People donated money to help the old couple, with some of them even sending signed, blank checks and telling us to fill in the amount! We got lots of mail from children who said their teachers were using this to instruct them about the meaning of honesty.

"One day I came in and saw an elderly gentleman sitting in the lobby. He told me he had read about the bank and had flown to Cudahy from some big city in Pennsylvania and wanted to talk to me," said Hal. "He took out some coins he had collected and said he wanted to leave them with me so I could get them appraised and send him the proceeds. When he started to leave, I told him I'd have to give him a receipt. He said okay and told me to mark on it, 'One bag of old coins.'"

Hal often spoke with his staff about the incident, pointing to it as evidence of how much ordinary people valued honesty and decency. Business also valued those qualities, he said.

"Business doesn't have to be underhanded to prosper," he said, observing that it could get along fine dealing fairly and honestly. "Sometimes, however, honesty takes the form of having to make a decision that isn't to the direct benefit of the business you're operating. But it's the *right* decision, just the same.

"In this case, we obviously could have turned a $6,500 profit for the bank in one day," Hal said. "There's no question that it would have been a legal profit. The question was, would it have been *ethical?*"

If he needed an answer, Hal Knuth got it from his bank's stockholders. Dozens called or wrote to comment on his actions; not one complained.

John and Ralph

Ralph Jones (left), Doyle McKinney, auctioneer, and John Fuson.

Having the respect of those around us demands that we first have self-respect, because we cannot be true to others if we are false to ourselves.

Two men whose self-respecting ways earned them the respect of their neighbors were John Fuson and Ralph Jones of Olney, Illinois. John, fifty-three, was a laid-off oilfield engineer. Ralph, sixty-five, was retired from the insulation business. Both had wives and grown families, and both were working part-time for a local auctioneer when the matter of respect came up in stunning fashion.

John and Ralph were sent by the auctioneer to the house of an impoverished older woman who was no longer competent to care for herself and so had been moved to a retirement home. Because of this, her house and possessions were to be auctioned in an estate sale. That's where John and Ralph came in; it was their job to sort through her belongings and get them ready for auction.

"We were clearing out a bedroom closet, sifting through things, when we found a bunch of quilts all folded up inside plastic grocery bags," said John. "We pulled out about a half-dozen of them before we reached the bottom of the closet, where there was one more.

"That one didn't feel like the others, though," he continued. "We unfolded it and saw this old purse. Naturally, we opened it."

"All you could see was money, just bundles of money," said Ralph Jones. "I've never seen so much in my life. There were singles, fives, tens, twenties, even a few hundreds. Lord only knew how much was there."

And it's likely that only the Lord knew what Ralph and John had found. After all, the old woman whose house they were in had lived a bare existence, hardly making ends meet, for many years before she had finally been disabled by mind-robbing Alzheimer's disease. This meant that the two men were alone with their discovery. It would have been simple for them to divide the spoils and enrich themselves by what turned out on a later count by the auctioneer to be $10,984 in cash. No one would ever have known about their windfall. No one except John and Ralph; but that proved to be a big exception.

"We sat down and talked awhile about what we should do," remarked John. "One way we could've gone was to keep it. There was always that temptation. But, really, there wasn't a whole lot of debate."

No one would ever have known ... except the two of them.

"That's right," said Ralph. "We agreed pretty quick that it wasn't ours and we couldn't keep it. My own way of thinking is that if you want to have something, you've got to work for it," he added. "I never worked for this, so it wasn't mine and keeping it wouldn't be honest. It would hurt my conscience, and I like to sleep nights."

John put it another way. "I've gotten along for fifty-three years without stealing from people, and I hope to get along another fifty-three the same way," he said. "Keeping it would have broken faith with the auctioneer, and I respect myself better than that."

John Fuson and Ralph Jones had a choice between riches and respect. They selected the path of true value.

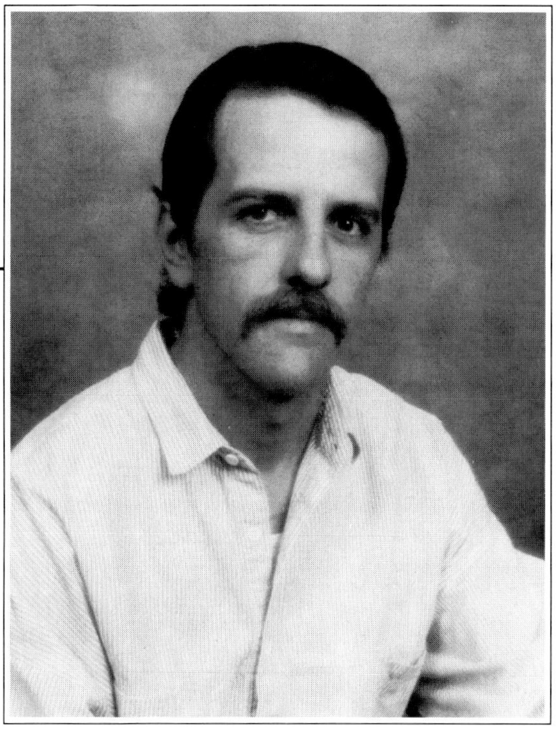

Kory Colvin

Is honesty absolute, or is it relative? Is it categorical, or conditional? Unequivocal, or circumstantial? Is honesty an all-or-nothing proposition? Or is it a comparative sort of thing, graduated and divisible by degrees?

For the philosopher, these questions might be open to debate. But Kory Colvin was no philosopher. He was an everyday sort of man whose uncomplicated view left no room for debate. It told him that either he was honest or he wasn't, and that he couldn't be slightly dishonest and still consider himself truly honest.

Kory, twenty-seven, put his opinion about honesty into action one wintry day in Pocatello, Idaho, where he lived with his wife and two young daughters. He was walking out of a parking lot when his eye was attracted to a gutter next to the curb. There in the snow and slush, something sparkled. He reached down and picked up a ring displaying one large, bright center stone surrounded by several smaller ones. "It's fake. Too big to be real," he told himself, glancing at his find. "Must be out of a Cracker Jack box."

He stuck the trinket in his pants pocket and started driving home, intending to give it to his daughters as a plaything. Finding it uncomfortably bulky to sit on, he pulled it out and tossed it on the dashboard. Just as he did so, he drove past a pawnshop, which inspired a whim in Kory. Instead of going straight home, he stopped and walked into the shop.

"Can you tell me what this is worth?" Kory asked, setting the ring down before a clerk.

"I figured she'd say it was glass, worthless," he noted. "But her eyes lit up when she got a good look at it. She said she'd give me $1,500 cash, then and there."

It was money that Kory had a real need for, since he'd recently wrecked his pickup truck when a car ran a red light. He had swerved and managed to miss the auto but hit a light pole, sustaining injuries that kept him off work for several weeks. So, temporarily at least, he was out of a truck and out of a job, though now it looked like he was in the chips with this offer from the pawnbroker.

He wouldn't be doing anything overtly dishonest, after all. He'd simply be selling a ring that he found on the street, fair and square. It could even be argued that matters were evening out for Kory — that he was having some good luck to offset his run of bad luck. Everything pointed toward his accepting the offer. Nevertheless, he turned it down.

"I told her, 'No, thanks,'" said Kory. "I picked up the ring and walked out, thinking that if it was worth $1,500 to a pawnbroker, it must have much greater value to whoever had lost it. I went home and called the police."

Officers were at Kory's door in less than five minutes. They told him that on the previous day, a distraught woman had reported losing the diamond engagement and wedding set that she'd worn for the past forty-three years. To her, it was irreplaceable, priceless; on the open market, it was valued at $15,000.

Now, it was right that Kory could have put a financial windfall to good use, "because we were in a bit of a bind just at that time." And it was right that he could have made all sorts of convincing arguments for the propriety of cashing in his good fortune with the pawnbroker. But what was not right was the feeling that would have accompanied that action. It would have felt uncomfortable, unwholesome, dishonest. For honesty isn't measured only by what a person *does*, but also by what he *feels* about what he does. If he senses in his heart of hearts that he's doing something even a little bit dishonest, then he must understand that no amount of arguing or rationalizing can ever make it honest.

"I knew I did right," said Kory Colvin. "It felt good."

The Glascos

Billy and Thelma Glasco with their son, Billy, Jr.

The truest test of honesty is temptation, since honesty without a challenge is a simple matter. Anyone can be honest when it's easy.

Billy and Thelma Glasco of Greenville, Mississippi, were honest when it wasn't easy. They were honest in the face of temptation.

The temptation that confronted them nearly fell into their laps one noon hour as they drove to lunch in Greenville. Glancing at a truck that was making a turn from a side street, Thelma, twenty-seven, noticed what looked like a canvas bank bag on the roof of the vehicle and pointed it out to her husband. Billy honked his horn and waved to signal the two men in the truck, but they kept going. The bag tumbled to the street.

"We stopped," said Billy, thirty-one, a sales representative for an acoustical firm. "I hopped out, picked up the bag, and handed it to my wife. We thought we might find some identification inside, so we unzipped it. It was full of money." The Glascos didn't know it, because they didn't count it, but they were holding about ten thousand dollars in their hands.

Billy and Thelma, the parents of a three-year-old son, looked questioningly at each other as if to say, "What now?" Thelma answered the unspoken query. "Let's take it straight to the bank," she said. "That's the only right thing to do."

No easy way out.

They noted the name of a local bank printed on the outside of the bag and drove to the nearest branch.

"We walked in and knocked on the door of this gentleman who was over the bank," Billy said. "When he asked if he could help us, I said, 'No, but you can probably help the guy who dropped this money.' 'Money?' the man asked. And I replied, 'Yes, sir, here's a bag full of money with your bank's name on it.'"

The Glascos gave their find to the banker along with pertinent information and were preparing to leave when the official said, "Hey, hold on a minute. Before you go, I want to shake your hands because I don't guess I'll ever meet two more honest people."

Not everyone responded that way, though. After details of the incident appeared in a newspaper, Thelma and Billy received some strange reactions. "We got phone calls from people who said we were crazy for giving the money back," Billy related. "One woman came right out and said, 'Folks think y'all a bunch of dummies. Y'all found ten thousand dollars and went and gave it to a bank. Don't y'all realize it was a gift from God?'"

"Well," he said, "I told her, 'There's no way in the world this was a gift from God. Why would God give us someone else's money?'

"No, this wasn't a gift, this was a test," he said. "There was enough money there to pay off every bill we owed. That could have been awful tempting."

Tested by a powerful temptation, Billy and Thelma Glasco took the hard way out. They resisted; they proved their honesty.

Jason Hill

Jason Hill, American superstar.

A story about honesty that hurt — hurt enough to bring tears — involved eleven-year-old Jason Hill of Sapulpa, Oklahoma.

Jason and his mother, Laura, were strolling away from a shop in Sapulpa one Saturday afternoon when the boy looked down and saw a wallet on the sidewalk. Barely breaking his stride, Jason scooped it up, slipped it in his pocket, and revealed it to his mom after they reached their car.

They checked through the billfold and found that it held $659 in cash, but no hint as to the identity of its owner. Jason tingled with anticipation at this information, since it meant he might claim the money for his own and buy a new off-road dirt bike motorcycle to replace his current one, which was out of commission for want of repairs.

Returning home with Jason, Mrs. Hill talked the matter over with her husband, Don. They decided that rather than tell their son what he *should* do with his find, they would ask him what he *wanted* to do. They would let Jason make his own decision. What the boy decided was to hold the money and watch the newspaper "personal" and "lost and found" columns to see whether anyone reported a loss. If it weren't spoken for within a reasonable time, then it would become his.

With the unvarnished candor of youth, Jason made it clear to everyone that he looked forward to keeping the money. And his hopes of doing so rose as the days passed and no one came forth to claim it.

Sometimes, it hurts to be honest.

Then one morning Don Hill phoned home from his place of work at an auto-body shop and told Jason he wanted to see him. The boy walked the few blocks to the shop and found his dad waiting with a newspaper in his hand. Mr. Hill pointed to a story boxed in red.

Jason slowly read and reread the article, which told about a local couple who had lost a wallet very much like the one Jason had found. They reported that it contained more than six hundred dollars in cash. They said they had intended to use the money to travel to Memphis so they could be close to their twelve-year-old son while he underwent medical treatment for leukemia.

"Well, what do you want to do?" his father questioned as Jason put the newspaper down and started wiping tears from his eyes. It would have made Jason look good to say that the tears were for the sick boy and his parents. But when he was asked about it later, Jason honestly admitted that although he felt sorry for the family, he wasn't crying for them. He was crying for himself.

"I wanted to keep the money—and wanted to give it back, too," Jason said. "I could have used it for a lot of different things. But I finally decided I should give it up, and I was sad about that."

As time passed, Jason's hurt honesty mellowed toward happy empathy as the boy with leukemia returned from Memphis and went back to school, seemingly in good health. "I was glad to think I helped him a little bit by giving back the money," said Jason Hill. "Maybe him seeing his mom and dad in the hospital made him feel better. I know if I was there, it would make me feel better."

Kay Shelley

The rule of the marketplace has always been "buyer beware/seller beware." Buy at your own risk and sell at your own risk. However, not everyone lives by this standard. Some answer to a different, more rigorous rule: the rule of conscience.

Witness the actions of Kay Shelley from Pinellas Park, Florida. She and her mother, Betty, were bargain hunting at an open-house tag sale one weekend when Kay discovered something that had the potential of becoming the bargain of a lifetime, if she abided by the rule of the marketplace. That she did not, bore testament to her honesty.

The tag sale was going on at the home of an elderly woman who had recently entered a nursing facility and was selling personal effects to pay her bills.

Kay, a St. Petersburg police detective, and Betty, a part-time hospital clerk, were browsing through some clothing when Kay's eye was caught by a red sweater she pulled from the bottom of a suit bag.

"I didn't notice so much that it was good-looking, but that it didn't feel right," observed Kay. "The sleeves were funny, hanging down farther than they should have been. I examined it and found a whole bunch of federal-government-type brown envelopes stuffed into each of the sleeves," she continued. "Every one of them contained cash, neatly folded in half, all in five- , ten- , and twenty-dollar denominations."

The garment in Kay's hands may not have looked especially attractive, but it displayed a very attractive price tag — $1. By plunking down a dollar bill, she had the opportunity of making the sweater and its contents her own, while at the same time making a sensational investment.

When is a bargain no bargain?

Yet it was an investment she never made.

Rather, she summoned authorities, sat down with a Pinellas Park police officer and the estate agent who was conducting the sale, and did a full accounting of her discovery, which totaled $8,340. The old woman whose home it was said her deceased husband must have hidden the money years earlier. Whatever the case, it made a nice surprise for her. But it just as easily could have made a nice windfall for Kay Shelley, if she had favored the rule of the marketplace over the rule of conscience.

"That's not how I was brought up, though," she remarked. "Doing that simply wouldn't have been right."

Kay Shelley might have ended her bargain hunting with a heavy wallet, but she chose to end it with a light heart.

NEIGHBORLINESS

What could ring more truly American than neighborliness? From the Pilgrims to the plainsmen to the present, life in America has flowed on a broad current of neighborly concern: people looking out for one another; people not just there but aware; people sensitive to the needs of those around them. People moved by kindly predisposition rather than proximity, since our belief has been that we need not live next door to a person to be a neighbor.

This hospitable, lend-a-hand spirit has left its imprint on many familiar themes in American life: battered wayfarers nourished and sheltered against the storm; needy individuals lifted out of despair by helping hands; nature-ravaged homes and farms raised from the ruins by the sweat of volunteers.

These have become recognized features of the American experience, markers on the map tracing our heritage as a neighborly people.

Marion Manwill

Marion Manwill delivers letters to rest home patients.

Marion Manwill was no stranger to this map. This Payson, Utah, high school instructor taught a generation of young people about neighborliness through awareness and sensitivity.

"One afternoon I was driving home on the old highway, from the next town over, when I approached a rest home that's just on the edge of Payson," Marion related.

"As I was coming along, I noticed this elderly gentleman, a nursing home resident, standing beside the road in front of one of those big, old-fashioned mailboxes — the kind you see mounted on the tops of fence posts. Well, he had the mailbox door open and was just standing there, gazing inside, kind of wistful-like," he continued. "To my mind it was clear what was happening: He was longing for a letter, and the mailbox was empty. I thought to myself, *I wonder whether shut-ins like that ever receive any letters*, because the old fellow just stood there and stood there.

"I could see him for a half-mile as I approached and in my mirror for a half-mile more after I passed," Marion said. "He never moved. He just looked into the empty mailbox. He seemed so lonely and forlorn standing there and probably thinking, *Gee, why don't somebody write me?*

"Something as poignant as that has a way of staying with you," he observed. "So after turning it over in my mind for a while, I went in and talked to the kids at school and told them that I'd been thinking about writing a few letters to the rest home patients, and maybe the kids would like to take part. They thought it was a great idea."

The young people Marion took it up with were members of his Payson High School Future Farmers of America chapter. They contacted the nursing home for approval, received an enthusiastic go-ahead, and launched a letter-writing program.

In the beginning, there were a few dozen students and just the one nursing home, with each student writing a letter a month to a designated person in the facility. With time, however, the project grew to include three nursing centers, a home for retarded men, and more than 120 students preparing at least two letters every month. Over a dozen years, they wrote more than fifteen thousand letters. In addition, they sent cards and gifts to the shut-ins for birthdays and other special occasions, and often visited them on important holidays.

"Some of the old folks were just Grandmas and Grandpas whose families couldn't take care of them anymore but did visit them sometimes," said Marion.

"But other residents, like some of the men at the home for the retarded, had never received a letter or had a visitor. They'd just been left there and forgotten, so these high school kids were their only connection with the outside.

"Even though the men were retarded and most of them couldn't read, they treasured the letters from our young people because they sensed that these represented human contact. A clergyman who visited there told me how the men would come up to him and say, 'Look, I have a letter from my friend. My friend wrote me another letter.' They would carry the letters around with them for months, until they wore out and turned to dust in their pockets."

Over the years, Marion said, hundreds of students — including the youngest three of his own five children — participated in the letter project before graduating and going out into the world.

"When I would meet them on the street, even years later, the first question my former students would ask was, 'Are the kids still writing letters?' They remembered it. It made an impression on them. I think it helped them to be good neighbors," Marion Manwill said.

"What's a good neighbor? Well, I think it's being involved with people and caring about them. People everywhere. I thought, and I always told the kids, that you can be good neighbors without living next door. You can be just as good a neighbor to someone from across town or across the country."

Charles Gonet

A certain man went down from Jerusalem to Jericho, and fell among thieves, which stripped him of his raiment, and wounded him, and departed, leaving him half dead. And by chance there came down a certain priest that way: and when he saw him, he passed by on the other side. And likewise a Levite, when he was at the place, came and looked on him, and passed by on the other side. But a certain Samaritan, as he journeyed, came where he was: and when he saw him, he had compassion on him, and went to him, and bound up his wounds...and took care of him...Which now of these three, thinkest thou, was neighbour unto him that fell among the thieves?

Luke 10:30–36

Father Gonet is interviewed by NBC the morning after the accident.

Charles Gonet of Springfield, Massachusetts, said he had always cherished the Bible's Good Samaritan message: Love your neighbor as yourself, and treat every person as your neighbor. Yet there was one aspect of the parable that never failed to trouble him: the part where the priest saw the injured man and passed him by.

"Why would he do that? Why pass by?" sighed Father Gonet, a Roman Catholic priest who came on the scene of a highway smashup one night and refused to pass by. He stopped: Two people survived because of it.

Father Gonet was driving on Interstate 391 near Springfield, heading home to St. Catherine of Siena Church, where he was pastor, when out of the corner of his eye he saw an automobile go into a spin in the oncoming lanes. "I thought at first it might jump the barrier into my lane, but it came to a stop first," he said. Slowing down, the priest saw that the errant car had skidded after colliding with a second one, which was on the hook of a disabled tow truck halted on the highway. A couple of people were standing next to the truck.

"My first thought was that they would take care of things and there was no need for me to stop," said Father Gonet. "I felt that don't-get-yourself-involved reaction flicker through my mind. But my heart told me I couldn't keep going. I hit my brakes and backed up. Then I saw that the car that had spun was now on fire."

The fifty-five-year-old clergyman hopped out of his automobile, vaulted over the concrete center divider, ran to the bystanders, and was told that there had been no one in either the stalled tow truck or the car it was pulling. So he turned his attention to the second car, the one that was burning. He could see nobody inside the heavily damaged vehicle but knew there must be someone.

"I went to the passenger side, the side that had taken most of the impact," he related. "With some effort I forced the door open. A young man was there, crunched down under the dashboard. I assumed he was alone in the car, that he was the driver and had been thrown across there in the crash. When I looked closer, I saw another young man also under the dash, on the driver's side."

Though both were severely injured, seat belts had saved their lives. But their safety was only temporary, since flames were rising from the motor, clearly visible through the shattered firewall between the engine and passenger compartments. If the men weren't quickly removed, they would burn. Charles Gonet vowed not to let that happen.

"They were wedged in under the dash, all tangled in the debris," he explained. "And they had injuries that I didn't want to make worse than they were already. One fellow had two broken legs, for instance. So I couldn't be too rough dragging them out of there."

On the highway, other cars were stopping, and onlookers were clustering in small groups. But no one approached the burning vehicle where Father Gonet struggled.

"The two injured men were semi-conscious, and I told them, 'You've got to help me get you out, because I'm here alone, and your car is on fire.' They tried. They attempted to push themselves away from the flames, but were so weakened that they just blacked out completely from the effort," he said.

"The fire was a foot or so away and growing fast. The wind was blowing hard, driving it. Eventually, I managed to work the passenger loose and pull him clear. Time was running out, though, and I doubted that I by myself could free the driver before the flames reached him," Father Gonet said. "I told myself, *This is ridiculous. I need help.* I turned to the people by the roadside and said in a loud voice, 'These young men are going to burn. Can't *you* lend a hand?'"

A Good Samaritan by choice, not chance.

The bystanders responded. While some took charge of the victim already removed, others joined Father Gonet in extricating the second one. And none too soon. As rescuers moved the two battered men away from their car, the priest heard a "whoosh!" and turned to see flames envelop the vehicle. In another few seconds, the injured men would have burned alive, and maybe their prime rescuer with them.

"These were two young guys in their twenties," the clergyman noted. "They had everything before them, their whole lives to live. With a possibility of getting them out, I couldn't have left them."

Father Gonet's will was strengthened by his long-standing sensitivity about the priest who passed by the injured man in the story of the Good Samaritan. "A thought about the Gospel of Luke just came to me when I stopped at the wreck," he said. "I used to cringe when I saw that passage and wonder why the priest didn't stop. I always felt uncomfortable whenever I had to read aloud that a priest had passed by."

In the next day's newspapers, one of which noted with unintended irony that rescue help had been rendered by a "priest who was passing by," Father Gonet saw the addresses of the two injured men, both of whom were strangers to him. "I realized that one of them lived just two or three streets away from this parish," he said with wonderment evident in his voice.

By chance, one of those he had saved was neighbor to Father Gonet. By choice, Father Gonet was neighbor to them both.

Marie Liu

Photo by Dennis W. Caldwell.

Life without an adequate home is the unfortunate lot that has befallen many Americans in recent years.

One of them, a woman of eighty-eight, lived in rural Jefferson County, Missouri, south of St. Louis. She resided in a ramshackle house by the side of a road, a place she had called home for perhaps twenty years. Though it wasn't grand (it was old and drafty and had no plumbing whatsoever), it was better than nothing at all. Yet she faced the prospect of losing even that semblance of a home when she returned there following a stay in the hospital and found that in her absence the dwelling had been condemned for lack of proper sanitation.

What did the future hold? Would she become a street person? Would she (more probably) end up in a public institution somewhere, forced to surrender her independence? That likely would have been the outcome of her plight, had it not been for her neighbors — a lot of Jefferson County people who didn't know her, had never met her, but cared about her nonetheless.

They found out about her through the warmhearted concern of Marie Liu, a young reporter-photographer for the Festus, Missouri, *News-Democrat.*

"I'm an optimist by nature, and I promised I would try."

"I was driving between assignments when I noticed a really old lady sitting in a chair on the porch of this dilapidated house beside the road," Marie recounted. "As I was passing, my eye caught a hand-lettered sign. It said something like: 'I want an old house to rent. This one is condemned.' This took a while to register in my mind. When it did, I stopped and went back."

Marie introduced herself and listened as the older woman described what had happened and how she had looked for another place to live but had found nothing that she, with her meager resources, could afford.

"I told her I wanted to help, though I wasn't sure what I could do," said Marie. "I didn't know if I could find her another place,

Marie Liu photo and story about Cora Mae Howell, shown sitting on the porch of her condemned house, moved people to help.

but I'm an optimist by nature, and I promised her that I would try. I figured the best thing would be to let other people know about this situation."

With her newspaper job, Marie was perfectly situated for that task. Snapping a number of photographs, she portrayed the woman's predicament in a picture story published by the *News-Democrat.*

"We started getting calls the next day," the reporter recalled, "from people saying they wanted to do all kinds of things to help." Marie found, however, that between the saying and the doing there was a wide gap, the bridging of which took plenty of hard work, initiative, and planning by her and others, not to mention a lot of money raised from the community.

But in the end, after seven months of frustration and false starts, the woman who had faced life with no home at the age of eighty-eight was moved into a big, good-as-new mobile home, complete with plumbing, air conditioning, and a full range of modern conveniences.

Along the way, her years of isolation were ended by the many neighbors she met and got to know. "That was one of the best things to come out of this," observed Marie Liu. "It's good to know you have a home, but it's even better to know you have friends."

John Phillips

Robert Frost observed that good fences make good neighbors. Perhaps that's a mildly cynical judgment, but it's one with a worthwhile point: Good neighbors are aware but not nosy, concerned but not pushy.

Yet where does a good neighbor draw the line between interested and intrusive? How is the difference decided?

Those were the questions that confronted postman John Phillips of DuBois, Pennsylvania, when he noticed a mail buildup at the home of a customer. A woman's life depended on John's answers and his neighborly disposition.

John, fifty-one, a husband and father, had been serving the same postal route for more than fifteen years. He'd gotten to know people's habits and routines in that time, and he made a practice of keeping an eye out for trouble.

He tried to be unobtrusive in this but wasn't always successful. There had been one particularly memorable occasion a few years earlier when John had spotted bills and letters piling up in the mailbox of an older woman and had inquired with neighbors, to make sure nothing was amiss. As it turned out, something was: The woman had been injured in a fall and was recovering in a hospital.

"When she got back home I was talking with her, mentioning that I'd been worried and had asked the neighbors about her," John recalled. "Well, she didn't like that one bit. She got kind of annoyed. She said she could take care of herself and more or less told me to mind my own business."

Now, here it was some years after that bit of unpleasantness, and John was seeing mail accumulate once again in the postbox of that very same woman.

"I noticed on a Saturday that she hadn't taken in Friday's mail," he said. "But you don't worry much about one day. Then it was still there on Monday and again on Tuesday."

John remembered full well the woman's warning to leave her alone, yet he was starting to worry. "As that Tuesday wore on, I thought more and more about it," he commented. "I could sense trouble. So at the end of the day I told my supervisor. He called the police."

Officers who responded spent several minutes knocking on doors and windows at the woman's home before they finally got an answer of sorts — a muffled groan from inside. They decided to enter through the front door.

"But they had an awful time," John recalled. "She had the place done up like Fort Knox. There were dead bolts, and locks, and chains, and bars. It took them forty-five minutes to get in."

When they did, police discovered the elderly woman sprawled on the floor with a broken hip. She had fallen in that spot five days before and likely would have perished there without John's intervention. Instead, though malnourished and dehydrated, she recovered in the hospital. With more than a little irony, she told the police that the one thing that had sustained her throughout her ordeal was the prospect that her mailman — whom she'd once told to mind his own business — would come to her rescue.

"You can't hold grudges," said an understanding John Phillips. "You have to keep in mind that people get old. Now and then they'll say things they don't mean. So you overlook it, take it with a grain of salt. I never really minded it. I was glad I could help."

The Simmonses

Like a pebble plunking in a placid pond, neighborliness has far-reaching effects — radiating gentle ripples spreading out and out, repeating again and again.

The ripple effects of neighborliness were seen and felt firsthand by Pam and Bob Simmons, who lived in the St. Louis suburb of Jennings, Missouri, with their two young sons, three-year-old Scott and eight-month-old Jeremy.

As with many families, the Simmonses enjoyed smooth sailing as long as things were on an even keel. But when a storm blew up, they were swamped. They got into trouble when the hours on Bob's truck-driving job were severely cut back, quickly putting the family behind in their bills. Pam wanted to take up the slack with a job outside the home but couldn't because Jeremy was ill and needed constant tending.

At the Simmons house, utilities were being turned off for nonpayment, and it eventually got to the stage where there was no food, either. At that point, Pam and Bob swallowed their pride and decided that she and the children would be better off in a public shelter than in a home without food or heat.

"The people at the shelter helped us straighten ourselves out, get back on our feet," said Pam. "And the experience of living there for a number of weeks opened our eyes to a whole world of needy people that we never even knew existed. They were people just like us, who never thought it would happen to them, but it did."

After a while, Bob got back to working full-time. Debts were paid, things righted themselves, and Pam and the boys moved back home. But the Simmonses carried a part of the shelter with them in their hearts. Awakened to the problems of others, they began volunteering at the shelter. Then, when the shelter closed down, Pam and Bob struck out on their own, converting their garage into a food pantry for the poor. They called it Neighbors in Need.

"When we were desperate, we were helped," Pam explained. "Now, we wanted to give some of that help back, to pass it along to others."

The Simmonses didn't have much money to give, but they did have time, so they gave that. Bob arranged his job so he completed his full week's work in three days, freeing him up for four days at the food pantry. Pam worked there seven days a week. Together, they collected food passed along to Neighbors in Need by much larger charities, plus that donated by individuals, and distributed it in an old van to needy families and elderly shut-ins.

"It's important that neighbors not close the door on people."

Presently, they were getting much-needed food to about 250 families and individuals each month. Several of these people later joined in to assist Neighbors in Need. "These individuals had all come to us previously for help," said Pam. "Now they wanted to become volunteers, to pass it on."

After more than three years of nonstop work, the strain began taking a toll on Pam's health. Hospitalization and medical treatment made it impossible for her to carry on. So the Simmonses passed the torch — Neighbors in Need — on to other capable volunteer hands.

But even as they did so, Pam promised that once her health returned, she and Bob would be back — this time not with a food pantry, but a full-fledged shelter like the one they had turned to in their time of need.

"It's important that neighbors be there for one another and not close the door on people," Pam Simmons stressed. "We have to be neighborly like people were eighty or a hundred years ago and just open the door when somebody needs something.

"If people would do that, nobody would go without and everyone would always have what they needed. We found that out ourselves. There wasn't a day since this all started for us that we didn't have what we needed. Maybe not always what we wanted, but what we needed. Help has a way of spreading little by little and bit by bit to the next person and the next, until it reaches everyone."

Like ripples on a pond.

Maurice Hellebuyck

"It was a real bad time for us. We never would have made it without our neighbors," said Maurice Hellebuyck, forty-two, of Mt. Clemens, Michigan, remembering a long-ago Easter Sunday when fire had destroyed his parents' home and everything in it.

"We had nothing left but the clothes we wore. No furniture or anything," he said. "But neighbors took care of my two sisters and me and put us up for weeks on end. They fed us and gave us clothes. Later, we moved into a converted three-car garage, and I can remember my dad saying that our neighbors had even helped us pay the taxes on our farm to keep us going. They gave to help us when they had almost nothing themselves. There's no way you can ever pay that back."

Nevertheless, Maurice tried.

When he grew up, he became a volunteer fireman and township constable. More than that, he lived by the rule of the helping hand: "When people need it, you give it," he said. "Not just dollars and cents, but time and talk and the willingness to be friendly with people." In short, he made himself the best neighbor he could be to those around him. Yet it was not in his own community, but in the nearby city of Fraser, that his efforts bore their sweetest fruit.

Maurice, a husband and father of five, was driving through Fraser when he heard a crash and turned to see that two cars had collided with such violence that the engine of one was knocked out of its compartment. It burst into flames instantly, threatening a mother and child trapped inside one of the mangled cars.

Grabbing the fire extinguisher he always carried in his own vehicle, Maurice sprinted to the crash scene and found himself shoe-sole deep in gasoline spilling from a ruptured tank in one of the automobiles. Although there was a gap of several feet between the fire and the fuel, he knew that one spark or wisp of flame would turn him into a human torch. Still, he didn't flinch. He stood his ground, used the extinguisher like the expert he was, quelled the fire, and pulled the crash victims to safety.

Sadly, the child died of her injuries. But the woman survived, prompting the Michigan Firefighters Association to cite her rescuer as the Michigan Firefighter of the Year.

Though it was not an honor he had sought, Maurice Hellebuyck accepted it graciously and with neighborly spirit. "All I knew was that somebody was hurt and required help," he would remark later in explaining what he had done at the crash site. "Anytime people have needed a hand, I've always done my darndest to give it. It's my way of paying back."

Bob Schaffer and Ed Braunstein in their market, and Ed delivering food.

Ed and Bob

Being neighborly isn't something that's limited to the individual. A business can be a good neighbor, too, by caring for and helping people even when it doesn't benefit the bottom line.

A business with a well-deserved reputation for neighborliness was the E and B Market on West Fourth Street in Mansfield,

Ohio. E and B was a grocery, somewhere between a corner store and a supermarket, big enough to be efficient and small enough to be friendly.

What made it friendly was the concerned attitude of its people, who took their cue from owners Ed Braunstein and Robert Shaffer, known to everyone as Ed and Bob (thus, E and B).

In an era of remote, automated, computerized, impersonal food marketing, Ed and Bob made a good neighbor of their business by taking a giant leap backward not long after assuming control of the store in 1982: They began offering phone-in, home-delivered grocery shopping to the elderly and disabled in and around Mansfield.

"Most of these people are in their eighties or nineties, all alone, don't drive anymore, and can't get out much," explained Ed. "But they're generally healthy and can live on their own, if they've got groceries. With our help, they don't have to give up their independence and go to a retirement home."

So every week, Ed and Bob and their staff would spend hours patiently taking and packing telephone orders for bread and milk and juice and frozen dinners and cereal and toilet tissue and light bulbs and whatever else was required to run a household.

Then, each Thursday morning, they would load up two trucks and head off for apartment buildings and homes throughout Mansfield, delivering groceries, and more.

"A lot of these folks are crippled up with rheumatism or whatever and have a hard time getting around," Ed noted. "So we unpack the stuff and put it in the cupboard or fridge for them." The people from E and B would also spend a few minutes at each of their fifty or so stops chatting with their elderly customers, making sure everything was okay, even doing small chores or errands for them.

What did Ed and Bob charge for this warm, considerate service with its origins in a bygone era? Beyond standard prices for the groceries, there was no additional charge in the beginning. But when the cost of liability insurance on their two trucks went up, they were forced to impose a fee: For those who could afford it, seventy-five cents; for those who couldn't, a thank-you would suffice.

"Hey, we do this to help people," remarked Ed. "The bottom line here is goodwill." And good neighbors.

Sean Wilson

Neighborliness isn't something that demands much involvement, much caring, or much of anything special. All it takes is a little more, a little extra, a little beyond the everyday minimum. The little things make good neighbors.

Such a neighbor was Sean Wilson of Lawrence, Massachusetts.

Sean Wilson accepts an award from Eagle-Tribune publisher, Irving E. Rogers, Jr., while his father and Eagle-Tribune circulation manager look on. (Photo by Ken Yuszkus, Lawrence Eagle Tribune.)

Sean, thirteen, was on his Lawrence *Eagle-Tribune* newspaper route one day, tending to business and hurrying away from a delivery he had just made, when his small qualities of neighborliness were tested—with a big effect.

"I heard this soft tapping on a window, and a faint voice," the teenager said. They were coming from the home he had just visited. If Sean were a less-concerned or less-helpful boy, he'd have ignored the sounds. But being the kind of neighbor he was, Sean went out of his way; he made a little extra effort.

Small deeds,
big differences.

"I went back to check," said Sean, who knew that an old couple lived in the house, which was just down the street from his own. "The husband was crippled and stayed in bed all the time. He couldn't walk or nothing," the youth noted.

As he returned to the house, Sean heard the voice of the old man who lived there calling to him from behind a closed, curtained window. The message was garbled, but soon became clear enough. "Can't reach phone," the crippled man was saying. "Wife on floor. Dizzy. Fell. Please. Must get help...."

The rest of the message escaped the boy, because he'd already heard enough to send him dashing to the home of a neighbor who had a key to the old couple's door. The neighbor phoned for an ambulance, then accompanied Sean back to the scene of the emergency. There, it was found that the crippled man's wife had had a stroke and collapsed on the floor, leaving her invalid husband unable to reach the telephone or help himself or her. She had suffered there for more than eight hours, even as her helpless mate had suffered watching her. And it's probable that Sean's little extra effort was responsible for her survival.

The boy, however, didn't make anything of it. He went off with his papers, never even mentioning the incident to his parents. The next day, as always, he was back delivering the *Eagle-Tribune*. Being an avid baseball fan, perhaps Sean that day turned straight to the sports section. Or maybe he looked at the comics. Whatever the case, as Sean's father would point out to him later, the boy went right past the front page without seeing that the newspaper, alerted by a neighbor, had hailed him as a hero.

Later, *Eagle-Tribune* publisher Irving E. Rogers, Jr., presided at ceremonies where the paper gave Sean a reward of five hundred dollars. "There aren't many real neighborhoods left today," said Mr. Rogers, "but Sean's concern proves that there still are real neighbors." Good neighbors, like Sean Wilson, ready to do a little extra.

AMERICANS AT WORK

... the best service that we can do
for our country and for ourselves:
To see so far as one may,
and to feel the great forces
that are behind every detail...
to hammer out as compact
and solid a piece of work
as one can, to try
to make it first rate,
and to leave it unadvertised.

OLIVER WENDELL HOLMES, JR.

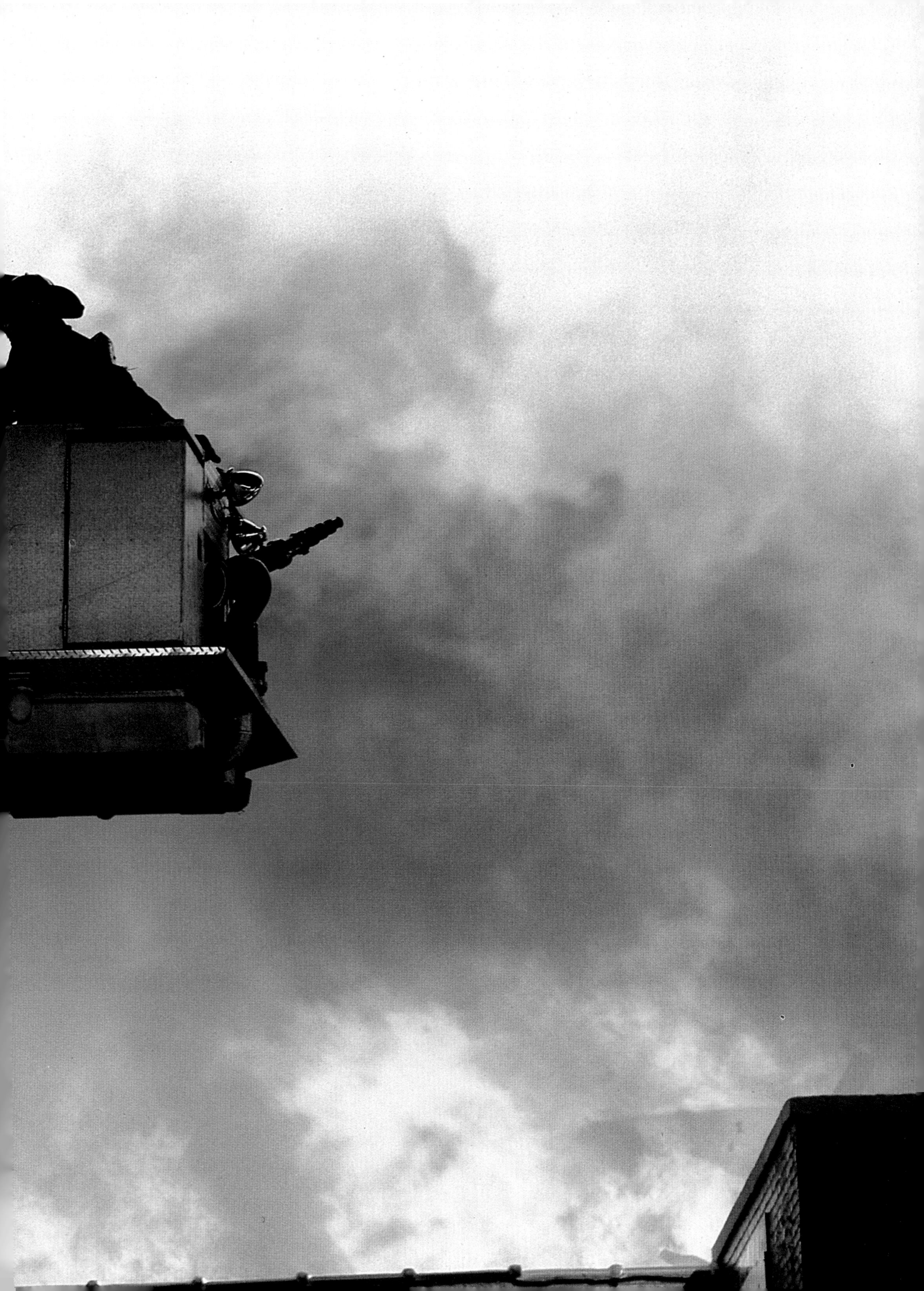

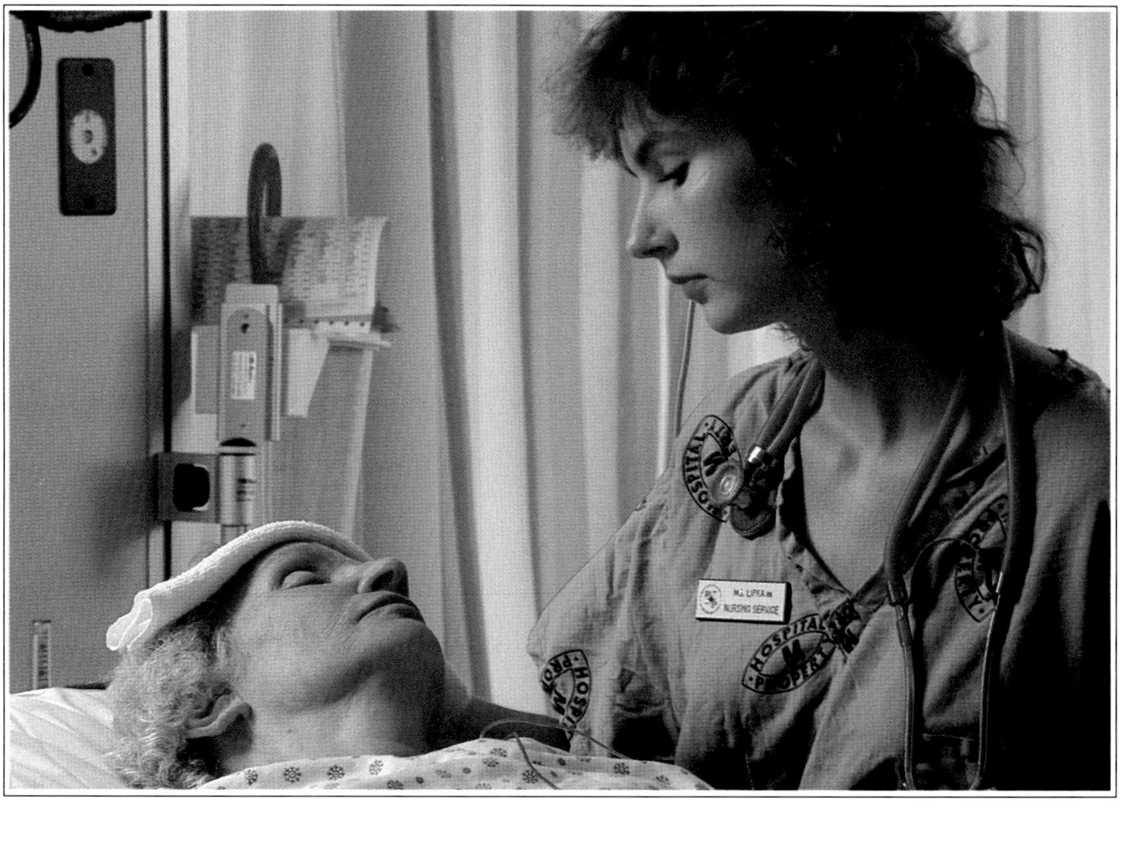
NURSING SERVICE
HOSPITAL
PROPERTY

NSTRUCTION

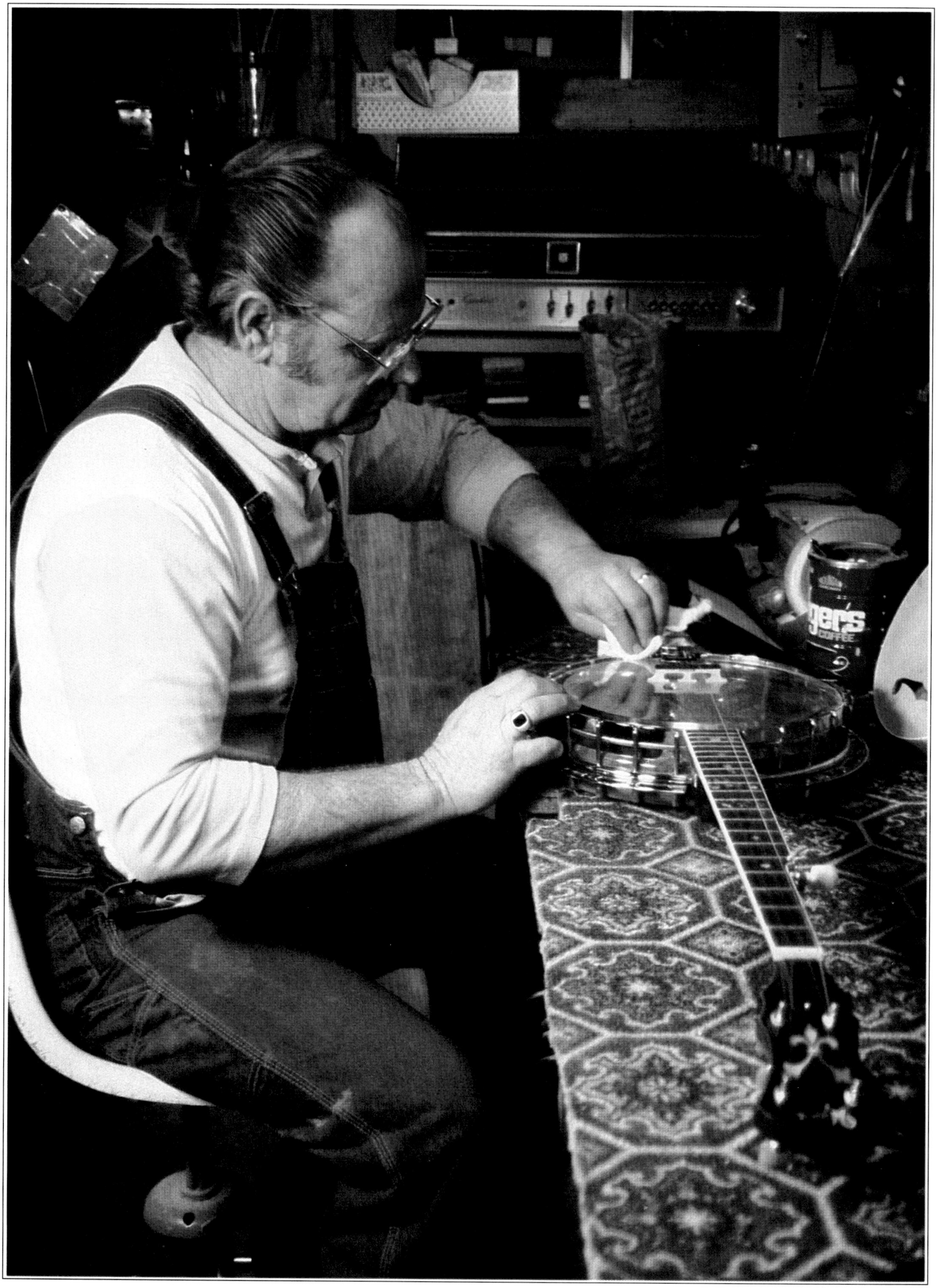
COFFEE

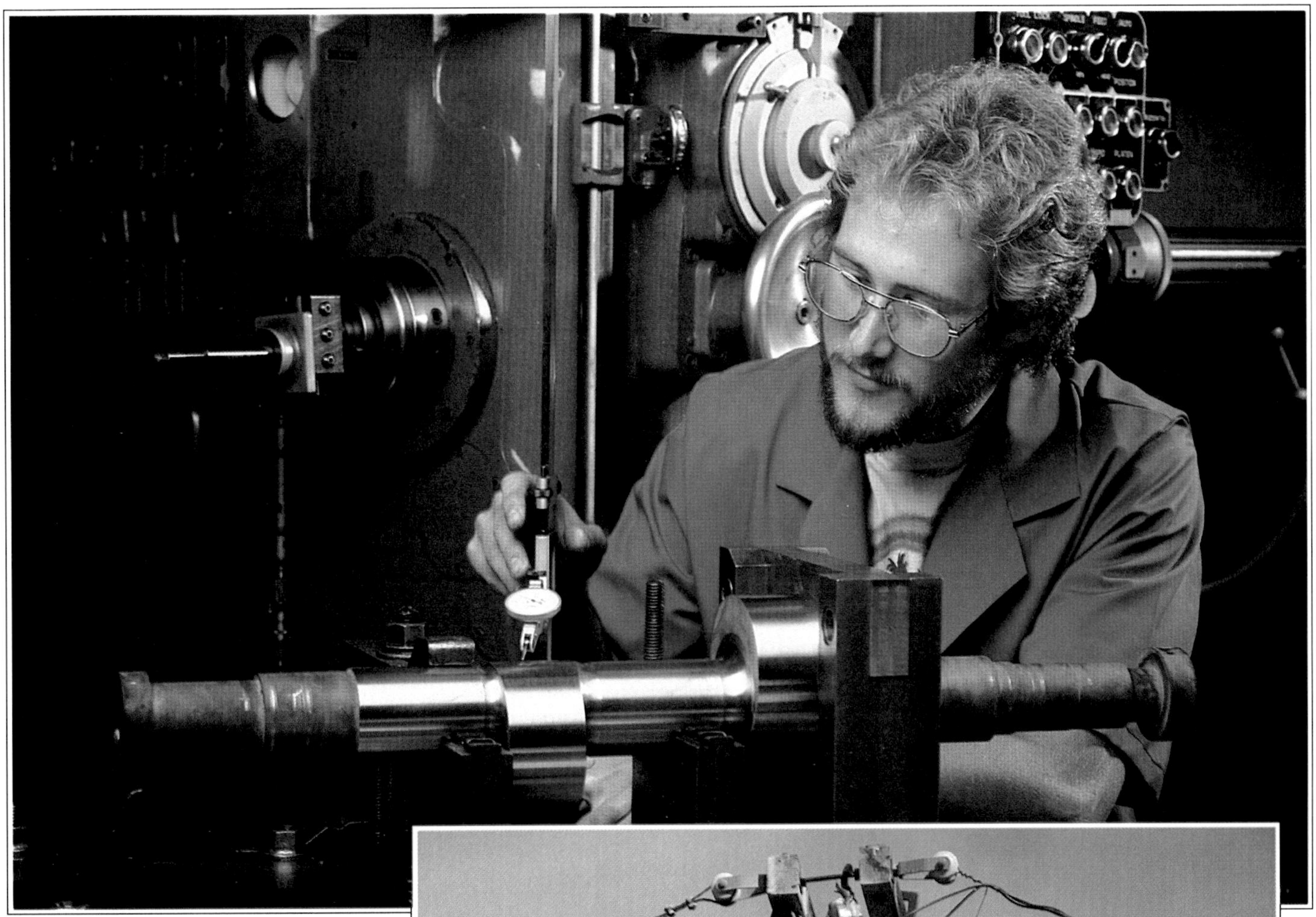

HONEY
CIDE

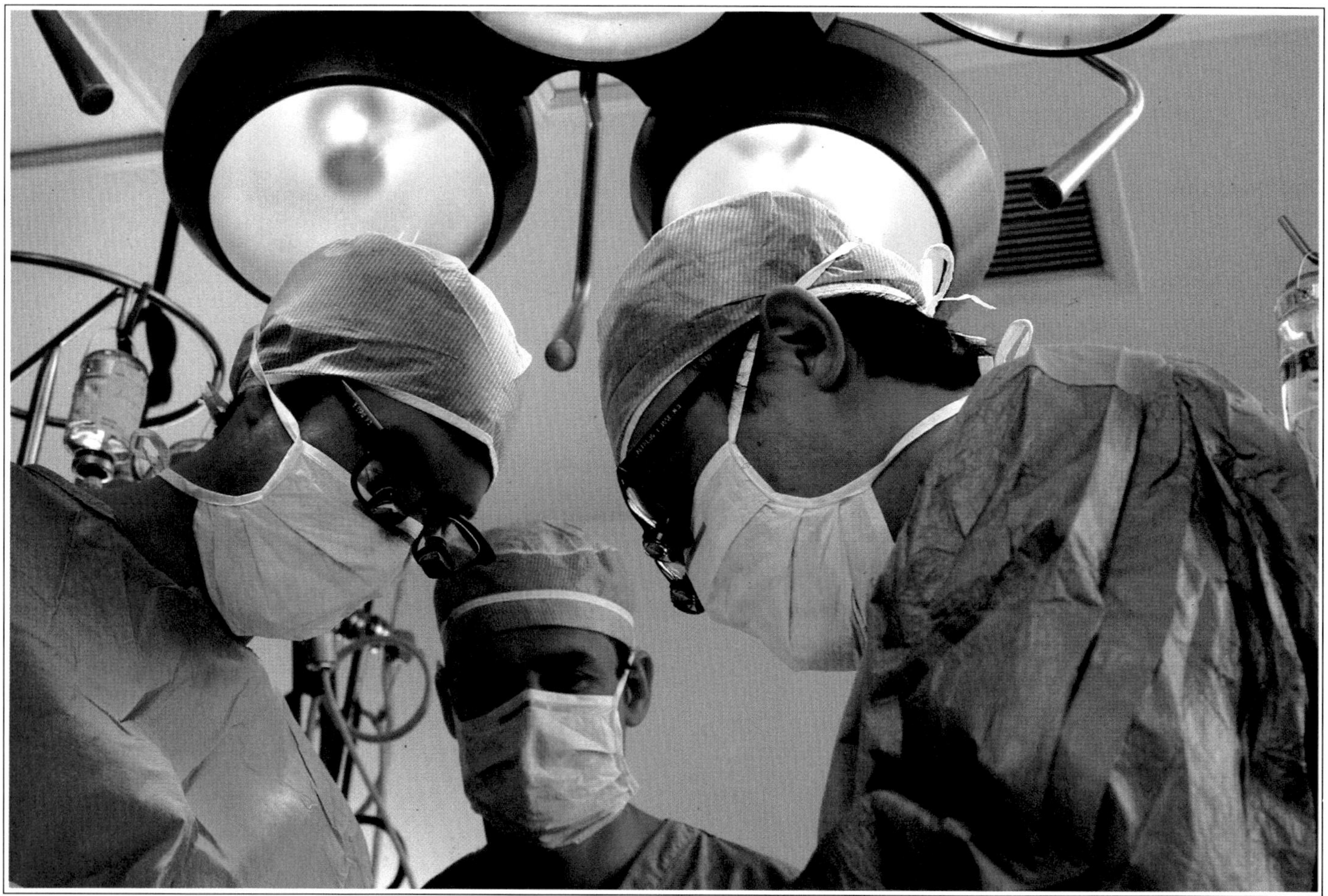

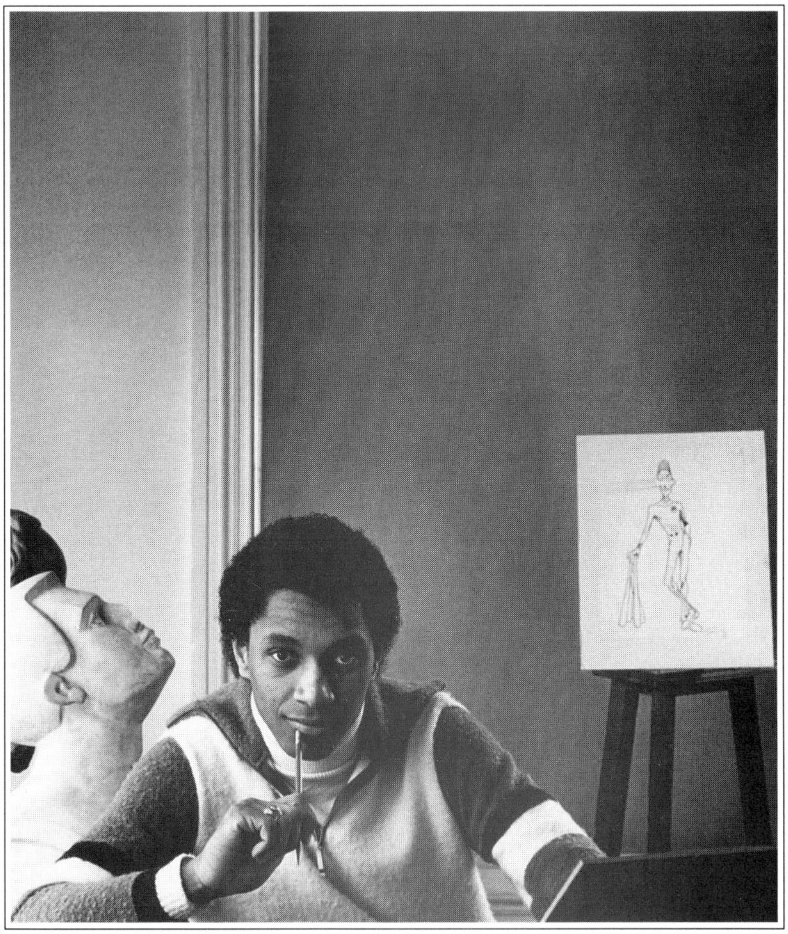

PENDRAY
FARM

MIEHLE
INK CORRECTIVE

Vienna Beef
TASE-D-HOTDOGS
PEPSI
ALL - BEEF
TASE-D-HOT DOGS
REG $1.00
JUMBO $1.50
POLISH $1.75
HOT LINK $1.75
TAMALE 1 50
COLD DRINKS 50
TASE-D-HOT DOG

obs&Justice
LABOR
Jobs&Justice
UNION Local 3
LABOR
Jobs&Justice
PRICE
UCSF

HANKO
JEAN SWITZER
FRED Leussler
PEACE
SCOTT
BEMIS
LARRY

HUMANITARIANISM

While it is a fact that Americans are tough-minded, and sensible, it's a fact as well that they are tender-natured and sensitive. They may *view* life with cold-eyed discernment, but they *feel* it with warmhearted involvement.

Americans are a humane people: compassionate, sympathetic, and understanding. They are touched by the vulnerabilities and sufferings of others and moved to relieve them.

There is little that can be counted on to evoke such an intense, immediate, and compelling response from everyday Americans as the sight of a helpless child, a hurting man or woman, a tormented animal. The sacrifice, tenderness, and gentle concern they readily extend in unselfish assistance testify to a vast reservoir of humanity in the American heart.

This wellspring of humane sentiment flows through our national life with purity and constancy; it bubbles from deep within the American character, continuously renewing us as a kindly and caring people.

Cynthia Daigle

Cindy Daigle, now postmaster, at the Gilman, Connecticut, Post Office Annual Picnic which she organizes.

The dashboard clock showed 2:25 A.M. as Cynthia Daigle headed to work, driving along a deserted road in the Connecticut countryside with silver sheets of rain rippling and swirling through the glare of her headlights.

In her solitude, Cynthia's thoughts meandered like the rural route she followed, moving from the three children she had just left safely tucked in at home, to the security she herself felt behind the wheel of her new car, to the demanding day's work she faced in her job as a clerk with the postal service.

Abruptly, all of her thoughts took wing, flushed by the shocking image of a man, arms wildly gesturing, who lurched unsteadily from the darkness onto the pavement before her.

"I saw this figure, this man's figure, coming from my left, waving frantically. He kind of jumped right in front of me, out in the middle of the road," related Cynthia, thirty-five, who lived in Oakdale and worked in New London.

"It was pretty desolate along there, and I normally wouldn't stop for anyone or anything and definitely not for a hitchhiker," she said. "But he had a look of desperation that seemed real. I thought there probably had been a car accident that I couldn't see through the rain, and that's where he came from.

"My window was cracked open just a slight bit, but of course my doors were locked and the motor was running. I backed up a little, because I had overshot him, and I asked, 'Is something wrong?'"

Cynthia recalled her reaction of disbelief when the man staggered up to her car, leaned forward, and whispered: "Somebody just slit my throat."

Looking closely, she saw that there was in fact a wound in the man's throat. "It wasn't gushing," she noted, "but it was wide open and bleeding hard."

For Cynthia Daigle, it was decision time. What would she do, a woman alone on a remote stretch of road in the middle of the night, confronted by a stranger with blood rushing from a mysterious gash in his neck?

"My first impulse, I must confess, was to flee. I wanted to drive on," she said. "A second impulse held me back, though. Something about his desperation, the blood, the whole scene, told me that this man truly needed help. But I wasn't about to get out of my car," she remarked, "because there could have been somebody else out there waiting for me. The newspapers reported afterward that I had gotten out and dragged him into my car, but they were wrong about that.

"I just said to him, 'Get in.'"

Making his way to the passenger side, the man slumped down on the front seat beside Cynthia.

"There was nothing I could do to help him because I wouldn't know what to do, anyway, so I took off for the hospital," she said.

"The man tried to talk but kept gurgling and choking on blood; it was running all over everywhere.

"He kept repeating, 'I'm dying, I'm dying.'

"That part was scary. Every time he said it, I stepped a little harder on the gas to get to the hospital and keep something really bad from happening."

Before they could reach the hospital, though, Cynthia and her wounded passenger arrived at the scene of a highway accident. It was ablaze with the flashing lights of police cars, fire trucks, and ambulances.

"I stopped and told the guy to stay put," she said. "Then I ran like crazy to an ambulance driver, dragged him over to where I'd parked, and said, 'I have a man in my automobile. His throat's been cut, and he's bleeding all over.' So a couple of emergency people took the man from my car, put him in an ambulance, and I followed them."

They soon arrived at the hospital.

"I was really worried about the man, so I went into this lobby area to wait for some word on him.

"That's when I just about fell apart," Cynthia observed. "My knees were like rubber when I looked in a mirror and saw what a state I was in. Of course, I hadn't even noticed in all the excitement. Blood was spattered all over me. I was completely red. My clothes, my brand-new coat, even my purse was covered with blood. So I was a mess," she said, "and the car was a mess."

But the man was alive, and remained so.

"A doctor came down to me in the waiting area after a while and told me that the guy was going to be okay. He said I possibly saved the man's life."

Investigating police officers echoed the doctor's opinion. They told Cynthia she almost surely had prevented the death of the man, whom authorities found had been slashed during an altercation involving two other men.

One lawman, while questioning Cynthia about the case, speculated that the victim would probably have bled to death or died of shock in a short time if she hadn't come to his aid.

"I told the policeman, 'If I hadn't stopped, surely somebody else would have.' But he just looked at me and said, 'Don't ever bet your life on it.'" When she reported to work about four hours later than usual, Cynthia found several of her colleagues in agreement with the police officer.

The man whispered to her: "Somebody just slit my throat."

"They said what I did was a brave thing, but they thought I was crazy to do it," she explained. "They said, 'That was pretty stupid, Cynthia. You could have got yourself killed.'

"I started getting mad at them.

"'Look,' I told them, 'the kind of thing that happened to that man could have happened to anybody. It might have happened to one of your relatives. How would you have felt if that had been your husband or your son out there and I had passed by and let him bleed to death? Ask yourself *that!*'"

A few hours earlier, Cynthia Daigle had faced the same wrenching question. And she had responded eloquently — not with hollow words, but humane deeds.

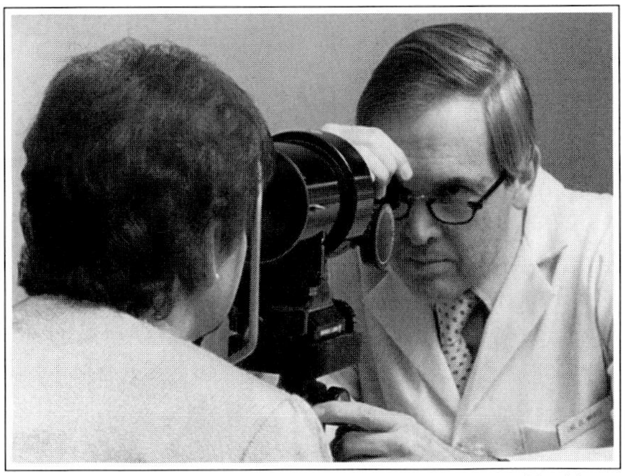

Dr. David White examining a patient. (Photo © by William Hubbard.)

David White

A man respected for his humanitarian treatment of the needy was David White, a physician from Lynchburg, Virginia. Dr. White practiced ophthalmology, or medical eye care, and it was his habit of providing this specialty free of charge to the poor that earned him people's regard.

It wasn't that he would treat an occasional indigent patient without fee. No. What set Dr. White apart was his decision to reserve one day each week *exclusively* for those who could not pay.

The day he chose was Wednesday, traditionally set aside by many doctors as their day off. But around David's office, it became one of the busiest days of the week.

That was the day Dr. White did away with fees and forms so he could care for the people he suspected were falling through the cracks between government-assistance programs: not poor enough for aid, but too poor to pay. There also were those who chose pride ahead of perfect vision and refused public assistance. David was disturbed at this prospect of people missing essential medical care simply for lack of money.

There must be many such in his community, he reasoned, and he attempted to find them in an unorthodox manner. One Sunday, after more than twenty years in practice, he ran this ad in his local newspaper:

I WILL SEE ANY PATIENT
FREE OF CHARGE
WHO CANNOT AFFORD
TO PAY FOR AN
EYE EXAMINATION
DAVID W. WHITE, M.D., F.A.C.S.
Wednesdays by appointment

Public response to David's offer was fast and affirmative. He quickly had appointments with about twenty patients for the first free session, and his Wednesdays soon were booked solid, months in advance.

"There was no 'means' screening of these patients," Dr. White pointed out. "I just put everybody on the honor system. And I must say, I was gratified to see that virtually all of them were truly in need of free care."

The few exceptions that came to his attention he did not worry about. "I would rather treat the undeserving for nothing," he said, "than have the deserving needy suffer."

For the most part, he gave routine care, attending people with flawed eyesight that could be improved with corrective glasses, which he prescribed. Then he persuaded local opticians to fill these prescriptions at cost or entirely without charge.

Now and then, he ran up against serious medical problems in his Wednesday patients — blindness-threatening diseases that would have gone undetected without Dr. White's aggressive efforts to reach the poor.

The profound satisfaction he derived from treating these cases gave David White his greatest returns from this humanitarian service.

But occasionally there were other rewards, as well. From some patients, he received a form of compensation uniquely appropriate to a specialist in eye care: grateful tears.

Frankie Mosteller

"I'm for the little people, the underdogs, the hungry and sick," said Frankie Mosteller. "My compassion goes out to them. I just care."

Against weighty matters like hunger and illness, caring might have seemed of little consequence. But on one desolate, rainy night, Frankie's caring packed just enough weight to tilt the scales of survival away from death, toward life.

Mrs. Mosteller was a fifty-three-year-old grandmother who lived in Conover, North Carolina, and managed a church-sponsored soup kitchen in the nearby town of Hickory. It was a job that paid her little but demanded much in the way of hard work, involvement, and caring. Especially caring.

Because caring counted with those who looked to Frankie for help. On life's ladder, they dangled from the bottom rung. They were the homeless ones, the wanderers, the down-and-outers, the people who had lost hope.

Though they came from diverse backgrounds, they shared at least two things in common: hunger and hurting. The hunger was physical: the gnawing of bellies empty too much of the time. The hurting was both mental and physical: While one side of life had beaten them up and left them ill and injured, the other side had beaten them down, crushing their morale.

They turned for relief to Frankie Mosteller, and five days a week, her soup kitchen put out a wholesome, nutritious lunch-all people could eat, and then some. But Frankie didn't stop there. She went beyond cooking, to concern — direct, personal involvement with folks in need.

One of these was a migrant worker named John. Homeless and in his late fifties, he slept in the woods and was a regular at Frankie's soup kitchen. When he failed to show up there for several days in succession, she grew worried and started asking questions.

"Where's John?" she inquired of some of the lunchtime crowd at the soup kitchen.

When they didn't know, Mrs. Mosteller checked that night with a few of the street people staying at an overnight shelter adjoining the soup kitchen. They told her that John was feeling poorly, had come down out of the woods, and was holed up at an abandoned filling station in town.

"He don't look good," one of them said to her.

Frankie took that as a warning and decided to investigate right then — that very night — to learn what had become of John. Being a woman alone, however, she was wary of going by herself to a deserted building after dark. So she prudently telephoned authorities and arranged for a police car to meet her at the gas station. Then she drove there herself.

Frankie arrived first, ahead of the police. In the cold, rainy darkness, she made out what looked like someone curled up within a pile of old clothes on bare concrete beside the building, which was locked.

"Is that you, John?" she called out, approaching the person who was huddled next to a wall for shelter. "John? John? It's Frankie, John. Do you need any help?"

There was a stirring in the heap of jackets and trousers and topcoats. "Frankie, I feel awful," said a weak voice that she recognized as John's. She drew nearer and heard him mumble, "My God, Frankie, I think I'm gonna die."

Indeed, he was near death. Frankie's gentle hand on his forehead detected a raging fever. "He was roasting, burning up," she recalled. "I'd guess his temperature must have been a hundred and five."

And that wasn't all. John hadn't eaten or drunk anything in nearly a week. Sapped by illness and hunger, he'd been unable to gain his feet or venture from that spot in several days. As a consequence, unrelenting diarrhea had soiled his clothes and left him in a disgusting state.

It required no expert to see that immediate medical care was essential if he were to survive. So when the police arrived, Frankie was all ready to lift John into the official car for a trip to the hospital. But an officer said no, it was against departmental regulations to transport any person not in detention, and John wasn't under arrest.

This left Mrs. Mosteller with a choice: wait goodness knew how long for an ambulance, or drive John to the hospital in her own automobile.

She didn't waste a minute.

Carefully loading John into her car and getting underway, she said, "I rolled down all four windows for ventilation, because he was in such awful condition — wearing three pairs of trousers, all fouled. He smelled something terrible. But that didn't matter, really. He was dying, and I had to get him help."

Making her way as fast as safety permitted over dark, rain-slicked roads, Frankie reached the local hospital in about fifteen minutes.

"At first, the people there told me they couldn't admit John," she said. "Some rule or other.

"They said I'd have to take him to the county hospital, ten miles away. I made a fuss about how sick he was and insisted that they accept him, so they changed their minds."

Physicians who examined John found him dangerously ill, suffering from pneumonia, a high fever, malnutrition, and dehydration. Although he was virtually at death's door, doctors who treated him in the hospital for a week finally cured him.

Yet it was Frankie Mosteller who saved him, with her concern, her questions, her sacrifices, her involvement.

"I have a heart for people," Frankie explained. "I realized that John was fixing to just lie there and die. I couldn't go home and sleep, worrying that this poor soul was out there dying on a stretch of wet cement, alone. He was in a dreadful state, sure. But he was a man — a human being — all the same. Besides, it didn't take much from me," she said. "Just a little bit of love, a little bit of care."

And a whole lot of humanity.

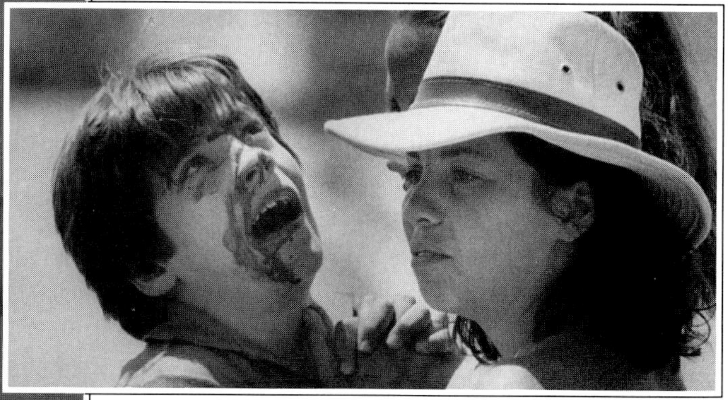

Michael Heller, aerial photographer, and photo of the accident victims which went out over the national news wire. (Photo © by Michael Heller.)

Michael Heller

This was a searingly dramatic photograph: a frozen image of human anguish that captured a young boy, face bloodied, eyes turned heavenward, mouth opened wide, crying out for someone to save his family from burning to death. It was the sort of picture that some photographers waited a lifetime for: an award winner.

Indeed, the man who took it did win a major award — though not for his photography, but his humanity.

Michael Heller was the man's name. By profession he was a news photographer, and by disposition a good and decent man, which the National Press Photographers Association recognized in citing Mike with its Humanitarian Award after newspapers nationwide published the photo he took and the story behind it.

Mike, thirty-nine, picture editor and chief photographer for the Santa Fe *New Mexican* newspaper, was driving back to Santa Fe from an assignment one Sunday afternoon when he saw clouds of billowing dust off to the side of the highway and suspected that a traffic accident had just occurred.

He was correct. A pickup truck and a tractor trailer had collided moments earlier. The pickup had spun harmlessly onto the median strip, injuring none of its occupants. But the big semi ran off the right side of the highway and down a steep embankment, where it overturned and caught fire. One man was killed outright, but four other people were still alive, trapped inside the smoldering tractor that had a sleeper compartment behind the cab.

Mike Heller hit his brakes, skidded to a stop in the roadside gravel, and told his girlfriend to flag down passing motorists for help while he sprinted to the crash scene.

An inspiring picture of humanity.

"The tractor was on its side, with smoke pouring out from under the wheel wells. The fire was crackling, starting to burn," he said. "I jumped onto the 'up' side of the cab and heard people groaning inside, like they were coming to after the crash.

"The door was open about six inches, but it was jammed so badly that I couldn't move it any further," Mike went on. "I looked through that slit down into the cab, which by now was filling with smoke, and saw a very frightening vision: the face of a little boy, illuminated by flames. When the kid spotted me, he started screaming, 'Get me out! Oh, please, get me out!'"

Just then, a trucker who had stopped on the highway joined Mike atop the burning tractor. Powered by all the desperate strength they could muster, the two men bent the jammed door aside far enough for Mike to reach down, catch the boy's collar, and pull him to safety.

By this time, several additional motorists had arrived on the scene with fire extinguishers. They controlled the flames while Mike and some others quickly dragged the three remaining survivors from the cab.

Only at that point did Mike leap down, grab a camera from his girlfriend, and begin taking pictures — one of which was the dramatic shot of the boy pleading for the rescue of his family. Unknown to him, it had already happened.

This photo and its details received close news media and public attention across America because of some recent incidents where cameramen seemed to have put pictures ahead of people. In one highly publicized episode, a man allegedly was permitted to set himself afire and burn to death while witnesses did nothing but record the event on film.

"A lot of times, photographers are criticized for concentrating too little on the victims of an accident and too much on the photos," Mike observed. "However, I think most guys in my business, and people in general, want to help. In my particular case, I got some pretty good pictures later, after I got involved first," said Mike Heller, a man who practiced photography some of the time, but humanity all of the time.

Kathy Wight

Kathy Wight of Largo, Florida, was a thoroughly modern American woman: busy career person, parent, homemaker, all in one.

Yet there was a touch of the traditional about her, too, reflected in her gentle awareness of people in trouble. Twenty-eight years old and the mother of two small children, Kathy knew that while her own life had its rocky spots, many others led lives that were much rougher. She did what she could to make them a little smoother.

This side of her character showed up routinely on her job as an emergency services dispatcher for the city of Treasure Island. Fielding calls that came in on the 911 phone lines, she made life-or-death decisions every day. As with caring for her family and home, she did it all in the line of responsibility and duty.

She made a bargain for life.

Beyond the call of duty, however, was her reaction to a series of medical-emergency alarms telephoned by an elderly couple to Kathy and other 911 dispatchers over a two-week period. On the first occasion, the husband reported that his wife was feeling faint. A few days later, she was having trouble breathing. Then, another day, she had fallen and he couldn't get her up. At last, the wife was admitted to a hospital for treatment.

But that did not end the appeals to 911. About a week later the husband made one final call, which was answered by Kathy Wight.

"He was really despondent," she said. "Evidently, he just was not able to cope without his wife. They'd been married over fifty years, and he didn't know when or if she was ever getting out of the hospital. She had always taken care of him, and now he couldn't care for himself. Then, of course, he missed her; she was the other half of his life, and he was terribly lonesome without her.

"So he called in on 911," Kathy remembered. "He said he was eighty-seven years old and all alone and didn't see much reason to go on living. He indicated that he had some sort of handgun and that he was going to shoot himself."

Following standard procedures, Kathy kept the man talking on the phone while she dispatched two police cars to his address, which she got from earlier emergency reports.

That was Kathy's professional response to the crisis: all business. Her personal response was something else: all compassion and humanity.

"I tried to draw him out on the phone," she said, "find out more about his problems. He said he had spent three hundred dollars in cab fares during the past week to visit his wife in the hospital. I'm not sure whether it was financial or what, but he said he didn't know how he was going to get to the hospital on that day, and he was desperate to see her.

"So what I did at that point was to bargain with him," Kathy went on. "I told him that if he would promise not to shoot himself, I would promise to stop over after work and take him to the hospital to see his wife. This seemed to satisfy him."

Indeed, police arriving on the scene a few moments later found the elderly man sitting calmly, without any firearms.

"But of course when he first phoned, I had to go on the assumption that he did have a gun," pointed out Kathy, who decided to follow through on her promise to visit the man, even if she had made it under duress. She finished work and drove to the apartment complex where he made his home.

"He was a little confused and thought at first that I was a cab driver," she said. "But when I explained things, he understood. I guess you'd say he was kind of crotchety or cantankerous — wanted to have things his way. Still, I found something really likable about him. I don't know, maybe it's because I have grandparents about his age.

"Well, we drove to the hospital, and the nurses gave him a wheelchair because he couldn't walk very well," she continued. "I wheeled him down the hall to see his wife, and it sure was worth the trip! The two of them acted like that visit was the best thing anybody could ever have done for them. He held her hand. She cried, he cried, and I could have cried without trying too hard. You just saw that there was a tremendous attachment between them."

With the visit completed and the old man's spirits restored, Kathy drove him back to his home.

"They lived in a small apartment, and it was, well, a wreck. It was a dreadful mess. I suppose it had gone downhill during the wife's illness and hospitalization," Kathy said. "This man simply had no idea how to fend for himself. Food was lying open everywhere, and the cockroaches were having a field day. The place hadn't been cleaned in ages. The laundry wasn't done. The bed linen needed changing. And there must have been three dozen ashtrays scattered around, all of them full, with cigarette butts overflowing onto the floor."

Kathy had already done her good deed for the day. Moreover, she was worn out from a full shift at work, and the usual burden of domestic responsibilities awaited her at home. Still, she could not bring herself to leave the old man in those conditions.

"He said he was hungry. I told him I would cook him supper but found nothing in the place worth eating," she remarked. "So I went out and got him what he wanted—thick-sliced ham and waffles. He refused to eat anything else."

While the man went to work on his meal, Kathy went to work on his apartment.

"I pretty much straightened up the whole place," she noted. "I cleaned and vacuumed and scrubbed, and changed the bedding, too. I did everything but the laundry, which I couldn't do because he didn't have any facilities right there.

"Then between talking to him and some of his neighbors, I found out that the couple had no children and that their closest relative was a nephew from up North somewhere, Chicago or New York," Kathy said.

"I phoned the nephew, who said he would fly down the next day and take charge of things, which he did. He arranged for the old couple to live in a nursing home together, so they could have constant care and be in good hands. I felt relieved by that. But before I left the old fellow, I got a promise from some of the neighbors to keep an eye on him until his nephew arrived the next day."

With that, Kathy Wight said good-bye and drove home. She had finished work at 3:00 P.M., and now it was past ten o'clock.

When someone inquired why she had gone to such trouble, involved herself, taken the responsibility to make life a little easier for two aged strangers, Kathy admitted to a soft spot for the elderly.

"My heart went out to these old people," she said. "I didn't think anyone else was going to react to their needs fast enough. But beyond that, I think one reason why people like me do these things, why we get involved and help other people with their lives, is because it makes us feel better about our lives," she reflected. "I've often thought, Wouldn't *everybody* feel better about themselves if they did a little more, went a few extra steps?"

In her humane concern, Kathy Wight wasn't satisfied with those few extra steps. She insisted on going that whole extra mile.

Michael Madera

In the climate of fear that prevailed, an expedient change in the rules by which people conducted their lives might have tempted some. But not Michael Madera. He lived by one central rule that he wouldn't change to accommodate fear or anything else.

"I try to be a decent human being," he said. "I pattern my own life so as never to make anybody else's life worse than it is, and if I can, to make it better," explained Mike, thirty-four, a Pleasantville, New York, father of three who drove a taxicab in nearby White Plains.

"This is a one-hundred-percent rule for me," he insisted.

"I can't be hurt by doing the right thing."

And he gave convincing evidence of that commitment one afternoon while at work behind the wheel of his cab. He was motoring along a street on his way to pick up a customer when he glanced toward a school he was driving past and spotted something that looked not quite right to him.

"I saw this real little boy tugging at the front door of the school," Mike said. "He seemed very small, and he looked like he didn't belong there. Then I noticed that he was crying, really sobbing."

The cabbie parked his car and walked toward the youngster, who cast a nervous eye at the stranger heading his way, then turned back to the unyielding door, yanking more frantically than ever. Mike saw that on the boy's back was a knapsack; on his face, a look of palpable fear.

"This kid was terrified, and just about hysterical," Mike recalled. "He was frightened out of his mind. Scared of his situation, scared of me, too."

Nor was it any wonder, for America was in the grip of a fearsome epidemic of missing children.

Every day, it seemed, from somewhere in the country came another horror story, a tale of disappearance, molestation, or murder more lurid and threatening than the last. Television, newspapers, mail flyers, milk cartons carried youngsters' photographs along with the ominous headline: "Have You Seen This Child?" National awareness campaigns warned children and parents of the lurking menace.

Families were not alone in their apprehension: Strangers who came into contact with children were regarded with fear and suspicion, and they knew it.

It was in this touchy atmosphere that Mike Madera approached the frightened and flustered little boy.

At first, the child was so intimidated by the big, dark-haired man who asked him his name that he wouldn't say a word. His mom and dad had told him never to talk to strangers. Eventually, though, Mike won the youngster over sufficiently to coax from him some sense of his problem.

"None of my friends are here," whimpered the five-year-old whose name was Christopher, "and I can't get in the school, and I can't go home 'cause my daddy left me and drove away."

In a flash, Mike realized what was wrong.

The door was locked, the school was dark, the playground was silent because this was a new legal holiday — the first year that the schools had observed Martin Luther King, Jr.'s birthday. This fact must have escaped the lad's father, who had driven Christopher to school for his regular afternoon kindergarten class without noticing anything unusual as he dropped the boy off and went on his way.

Christopher had stood crying at the bolted door for perhaps twenty or thirty minutes. How much longer he would have stayed, or what might have befallen him if he had lingered there alone, became only matters of unhappy conjecture once Mike Madera arrived on the scene.

Having gained the boy's reluctant confidence, Mike was surprised to learn that Christopher could recite his home address. This provided a simple solution to the problem, Mike thought: All he had to do was drive the child home, and that would be the end of it. But it didn't work out that way, since when they arrived at Christopher's place, no one was there. Nor was any nearby neighbor home.

Dead-ended in those two efforts, he put Christopher back in the cab and drove to a police station.

There, Mike got a sobering reminder of just how potentially risky his actions had been. Streetwise officers, unready to accept at face value the cabbie's account of what had happened, interrogated him very closely on all points. As Mike put it, only half-jokingly, "They cross-examined me to see if my story checked out."

It did check out, and authorities reunited Christopher with his father.

Clearly, though, one offhand comment or verbal misstep by Mike could have left him open to all manner of shocking charges and landed him in a lot of trouble. He would not have been the first well-meaning passerby to get a bad return on good intentions.

Even so, this was a peril that Mike could easily have avoided, one he might literally have steered clear of by simply driving past the school without stopping. Or, having paused to learn what was wrong, he could have reported the matter to police via his cab's two-way radio and then gone about his business.

In the climate of fear that existed, this expedient concession to hard reality might have merited some consideration, yet Mike gave it none. Why?

"My thoughts and actions were all based on the safety of this little boy," he said. "Obviously, I couldn't leave him out there, in light of the kinds of things that can happen to children. If somebody's going to accuse me of something for doing this, then that's how it is. But I really believe that I can't be hurt by doing the right thing. I don't think I can possibly hurt myself by being a Good Samaritan, but I might hurt myself by being a bad Samaritan," said Mike Madera.

"I did only what I should have done as a decent human being. Nothing more."

Surely, nothing less.

Mary McBride

"All living creatures deserve our humane respect," observed Mary McBride. "Even if they're not speaking creatures, they are feeling creatures. And I can't allow any of them to suffer," added Mary, who spoke of gentle regard not only in words but also in deeds, even when her deeds meant sacrifice and personal peril.

Ms. McBride, forty-eight, a retired air force nurse, lived on the shore of Johnson Bayou in Panama City, Florida.

She was doing some yard work one day, "just puttering," as she put it, when she became aware of a dog barking from the area of her neighbor's house. After a few moments, the persistent yapping began to trouble Mary. It wasn't long before she realized why: Her neighbor didn't *own* a dog.

"So I walked around onto the dock to see where the barking was coming from," she said. What she saw was a little dog, yelping frantically, swimming round and round about thirty yards out in the bayou, which was a tidal body of salt water.

"There would have been no trouble for him at low tide," Mary pointed out, "because the beach is exposed then. But the tide was in, the beach was covered, and he couldn't get up over the seawall.

"He was barking for help."

And the woman tried to give him help. She reached out and called to the animal, which at first swam toward her. But then, unaccountably, it turned about and paddled away, moving farther out into the bayou, which was about thirty-five-feet deep.

Mary had two options: look for somebody else to come along and attempt a rescue, or try on her own to save the dog, whose barking grew weaker with the passing moments.

"To me," she said, "that wasn't much of a choice. This little creature was out there drowning. Whether it was a kid or a dog or a cow, I'd have done the same thing. I didn't see any recourse except to go in after him.

"I dived in and swam in his direction. He was still moving away, but much more slowly," Mary continued. "As I approached, he sank under the surface once, then came up and sank a second time. He was submerged when I got to him, and I don't think he'd have come up again. I pulled him up and he didn't struggle at all. He was just about dead, drowned. When I got him ashore, he was so puffed up he could hardly breathe. His poor little belly was like a balloon."

Without even stopping to dry herself or change clothes, Mary set off for the veterinarian's office, holding the dog on her lap during the drive. "When we got there," she chuckled, "I went squishing and sloshing in and gave him to the vet to work on, then went back outside and poured the water from my shoes."

The doctor explained that the dog, in its panic, had gulped so much air that it had inflated its stomach to the point where the stomach pressed on the animal's lungs and impaired its breathing. To deal with this, the vet used a needle to poke a series of holes that deflated the stomach.

With that accomplished, the dog was put in care of the Panama City Animal Shelter. After some searching, the shelter located the creature's owner, who said that her pet — a twelve-year-old schnauzer named Tobie — was in frail condition and seldom went near the water. It was speculated that he had wandered down to the seawall and fallen off.

By whatever manner Tobie came to the point of drowning, all agreed that Mary had saved him, although she denied suggestions of heroism on her part. "I'm a pretty good swimmer," she explained, "and this little fellow was drowning."

But it was a different matter when Tobie's owner praised Mary McBride as "a great lover of animals." That, Mary could not deny.

Brian Koenig

"Straight out of the 'Twilight Zone,'" Brian Koenig was saying, wonder still evident in his voice long after the experience. "It was so unreal, so shocking, that for an instant it was incomprehensible to me. I couldn't make sense of what I was seeing."

Brian, thirty-six, a Milwaukee, Wisconsin, insurance underwriter, explained that he'd been driving along Interstate 94 in Milwaukee one Sunday evening when "something white, a white bundle" appeared suddenly, tumbling and rolling on the pavement ahead of him.

"At first I thought it was a dog," he said. "It was on the right side of the road, and I was just changing from the right to the center lane. I was almost on top of it when I saw two tiny legs sticking out. It was a child! It took my breath away," Brian said. "I couldn't imagine where it had come from. That's the last thing you'd ever expect to see lying on the interstate."

Shaking himself free of the "Twilight Zone" and back into harsh reality, he quickly responded, pulling his car to a panic stop at the roadside and leaping out.

"There was heavy traffic — everybody coming home from the summer weekend," he said. "I had to get back there quick, before somebody in the right lane drove over the child.

"I ran harder than ever in my life," recalled Brian, who dashed not along the shoulder of the three-lane, northbound section of the highway, but in the right lane itself. "I was sprinting into the traffic, waving my arms, trying to move them off from the right side of the road toward the middle.

"When I got there, I saw it was a little girl. Her head and right arm were resting on the white line at the edge of the road, and her body was in the highway, about where the right wheels of a car would hit," he went on.

"I thought for sure she was dead. But I got down on my knees to check. The cars were passing a couple of feet from me, and I could feel the wind as they rushed by. I went on waving traffic away with one hand, and with the other I felt for a pulse in the child, who looked about two years old and was all rolled up in a long white dress," Brian observed.

"After what seemed like about a minute, she breathed this small sigh. I realized she wasn't dead, but unconscious. Fortunately, some other motorists were stopping. They got themselves out in the lane and flagged the traffic aside. To be safe, though, I had to move the child off the road. Very carefully, I shifted her toward the shoulder of the highway.

"She was coming back to life, so to speak, on the side of the road. She started to move, and I had to restrain her, to protect her from hurting herself more than she was already. I wasn't certain, but I guessed that she was badly injured."

In fact, the youngster, who had accidentally tumbled from her family's camper van at highway speed, was near death with a fractured skull, a broken arm, and other injuries.

Before long, medics made their way through traffic and sped her to the trauma center at St. Luke's Hospital.

As the ambulance screamed into the distance, Brian Koenig climbed into his car and drove quietly away, his efforts unknown to the world at large. And they would have remained unknown had he not been such a caring person. Concerned that the child's family, traveling in a camper, could have been from out of town with no place to stay, he stopped at St. Luke's on his way home, to offer her parents accommodations or anything else they might need.

It turned out that they had a home in the Milwaukee area. But before Brian could get to the family and find that out, news reporters got to Brian, intercepting him on his way into the hospital and asking so many questions about the accident that he lost his chance to meet the girl's parents.

By coincidence, however, he got a second chance.

After doctors initially treated the youngster at St. Luke's, they sent her to receive specialized child care at Milwaukee Children's Hospital. And it was there that her parents and Brian Koenig met the very next night, Monday, which was Brian's regular time for volunteering at Milwaukee Children's.

"It was a child! –the last thing you'd expect to see lying on the interstate."

"Once a week I spend an evening in the waiting area of the intensive care unit at Children's, mainly comforting and attending parents whose kids are critically ill there," he noted. "For the most part, I simply talk with parents, sharing their feelings and fears."

In addition to volunteering at Children's Hospital, Brian also involved himself in the Big Brother program, sharing love and companionship with a fatherless thirteen-year-old boy.

Brian had taken up those child-oriented activities, he explained, "to fill an emptiness in my life and also to remember my son," four-year-old Brendan, who had died two years earlier in a room at Children's Hospital just down the hall from where Brian chatted with the parents of the little girl.

Unlike her, Brendan had been a victim not of injury, but illness — a rare childhood disease that took his life in a matter of days.

"I was so devastated watching my son die," Brian said. "As a parent, you want to do anything you can to protect them, nurture them, give them a bright future. There wasn't anything I could do for Brendan, though. I felt so helpless."

But he said it was a different story that Sunday evening with the little girl lying crumpled on Interstate 94.

"As I knelt down over her, I thought of Brendan and my helplessness with him," Brian poignantly recalled. "I was determined that if I had anything to do with it, this child would not die."

Happily, she did not.

The little girl recovered completely, thanks both to the skilled physicians who treated her catastrophic injuries, and the caring man who kept those injuries from becoming even worse.

For that, newspaper headline writers hailed Brian Koenig's heroism. And in truth, he was a hero: kneeling on the freeway amid the high-speed traffic, risking his life, shielding her defenseless body with his own.

But more than a hero, he was a humanitarian — someone concerned with the welfare of people, *all* people.

"I didn't know who this little girl was, but she needed my help," Brian said. "And when a person's in need, you help them as though they were somebody very close to you. You've got to treat strangers and everybody like they were family."

Brian Koenig's family was all the world's family: the family of Man.

INITIATIVE

Initiative — the bold, resourceful spirit of enterprise — is a hallmark American trait. After all, wasn't this the essential characteristic that fueled America's discovery, exploration, and settlement? Surely, it was. Just as surely, it was this same spontaneous quality that energized the fantastic accomplishments of America's premier inventors, scientists, industrialists, and developers. Those famous men and women became world leaders and world beaters by seizing the initiative and determinedly achieving their goals in the face of daunting obstacles.

Less dramatic but equally as evident has been the practical initiative of unsung, everyday Americans. For the essence of initiative is action, and it is well recognized that Americans, individually and collectively, have seldom been much inclined to passivity. Faced with problems or crises, their disposition has been to act. If something needed fixing, they fixed it. If something needed changing, they changed it. If something needed doing, they did it, refusing to be discouraged by circumstances and looking not to others but to themselves for the resources to see a task through.

For more than two centuries, initiative has been the spark firing the engine propelling the American people and nation continuously forward. It is a spark that flashes as brightly today as ever in our history.

Dewayne Carter

Dewayne Carter of Edmond, Oklahoma, was a contemporary American in whom the spark of initiative shone brightly. Because of that, the spark of life shone brightly in another man.

Dewayne, forty-three, was dining out with two of his grown sons, their wives, and his own wife at an Edmond steak house one evening when his attention was caught by a commotion at another table.

"I thought at first it was a fight," said Dewayne, the operator of a convenience store in Edmond. In a way, he was right: It wasn't a fistfight, but it was a fight for life. A middle-aged man had choked on a piece of steak and begun clutching at his throat, prompting those around him to rush to his aid.

The situation seemed to call for the Heimlich maneuver that is used to clear blocked airways. So one by one, three different men familiar with that procedure circled their arms around the stricken man from behind, knotted their hands below his diaphragm, and jerked repeatedly upward and inward, attempting to force out the obstruction. One by one, each of the would-be rescuers failed as the man lapsed into unconsciousness and slumped slowly toward the floor.

With the crisis deepening, about two dozen people had gathered round, first drawing near, then pulling back little by little and growing silent as the successive resuscitation efforts came to naught. It seemed evident that if the man were to survive, a different approach would be needed. But what?

"You're going to have to 'trake' this guy," announced Dewayne Carter as he stepped forward out of the crowd. Dewayne's "trake" reference was to the surgical procedure known as a tracheotomy, where an emergency airway is created by cutting a hole at the base of the victim's throat, allowing the windpipe to be opened below the point of obstruction.

His radical initiative paid off.

"I was convinced that this man was in big trouble," said Dewayne. "Three guys who knew what they were doing had tried and failed with the Heimlich. So whatever he had choked on was really stuck in his throat, and he had been without oxygen for three or four minutes. If it went on much longer, he would be dead or brain damaged. As it was, he had no pulse, was all frothed-up at the mouth, and his face was a deathly shade of gray-black."

This suggestion of a tracheotomy was a radical initiative, and one of the men attending the choking victim turned to Dewayne and asked, "Do you know how to do it?"

"I think so. I've never done it, but I've seen it done, and I think we ought to try," he responded. Dewayne didn't mention the long-ago combat incident in Vietnam when, as a navy signalman, he had watched a corpsman on the deck of an American gunboat do a tracheotomy on a wounded serviceman while enemy fire tore the air overhead. That scene had burned itself vividly into Dewayne's memory, and now, he recalled it.

Positioning the dying man faceup on the floor, Dewayne knelt next to him and grabbed an unused steak knife. He tried to cut a vertical slit in the man's throat, but the utensil was too dull, and he called for something sharper. The restaurant proprietor handed him a finely honed butcher knife.

"I held it so that only about an inch of the point extended from my right hand," he explained. "I steadied it with my left hand and made a vertical cut through the muscle and cartilage. There was almost no blood.

"I pushed my little finger through this slit," he continued, "and hollered at my son to get me a straw, which I inserted and blew into while I pounded on the guy's chest. Almost immediately, a girl who'd been checking his wrist said, 'I've got a pulse! His heart's beating!'

"I'm no surgeon, so this was no textbook procedure," said Dewayne, slowly reflecting on the life-or-death events at the steak house. "But it worked out, just the same. Without this, I figured he would die for sure. And I wasn't going to stand there and see that happen without at least trying."

Dewayne's approach to this crisis turned out to be more than radical. It was rewarding, too: The man he operated on recovered completely and came to appreciate that each bright new morning of his life was a tribute to Dewayne Carter's initiative.

John Dillon (left) outside the Chrysalis Clothing Center.

John Dillon

A marvel of nature is the chrysalis, the stage of development during which caterpillars turn into butterflies. This wondrous transformation from homely, hairy, crawly creatures into delicate, colorful, winged beauties occurs altogether naturally and effortlessly. A chrysalis that did not happen with such natural ease, however, was the one which appeared in the skid row district of Los Angeles. That chrysalis was born entirely of the initiative and struggle of John Dillon.

John was just twenty-two when he turned up on Los Angeles's skid row. A recent university graduate and the product of a comfortable middle-class upbringing, it was choice, not chance, that brought him to that seedy area of tenements and missions, derelicts and drifters that he spoke of as "ground zero" because the human devastation there reminded him of the physical devastation found at the point of a nuclear blast.

"For lack of a better word, you could call skid row people the 'outs,'" said John, a slender young man with glasses. "They were out of doors — homeless; out of luck; out of confidence; out of prospects; out of faith; out of hope." But John believed they were not out of reach. He believed with the right approach, they could be helped.

"These were very poor people," he said. "They weren't like me and didn't have the advantage of my background, but they were interesting and pleasant. I liked them. I respected them. I cared about them. I told myself, *I can step in here and get something going to alleviate the suffering and pain in their lives.*

"All through college, my friends and I had talked about doing something to solve the world's problems, like the problems of the poor," he went on. "When I saw what was happening on skid row, I knew it was time to stop talking and start doing."

The young man explained that when he traveled to Los Angeles from his Maryland home a few months earlier, he had intended to work as a volunteer in a private welfare agency. "I'd planned to do that for about a year," he said, "after which I would take a trip to Europe before starting law school.

"Instead, I quit my volunteer position," John said, "and took the money I'd saved for Europe and used it to start changing things on skid row.

"Just about all of my $3,000 was gone in the first month. I rented a place and wrote a rent check for $1,200 against a balance of $1,200.07. After that, my budget was a penny in and a penny out. The place I rented and set up shop in had been one of the toughest bars on skid row. Before it was shut down, it was called the Hard Rock Café."

John renamed it the Chrysalis Center, reflecting his hope that it might somehow help a few skid row inhabitants transform their lives — take wing and fly away from there.

"I didn't have any grandiose plans," he said. "I just wanted to address people's basic needs: clothes, food, and the like.

"But I wanted to do it differently from the way I'd seen it done before," he pointed out. "It had struck me that relief agency workers seldom if ever asked the people who came to them for help what it was *they* wanted. The workers would just say, 'Here's some soup' or 'Your cot is over there.' They wouldn't sit down with people and say 'What do you *really* want?'"

In the early going, John and the Chrysalis Center helpers he recruited didn't have a great deal to offer, just some words of encouragement and used clothing to be given away. Still, the homeless, the destitute, the down-and-out who ventured there appreciated the help. Arriving with tattered clothes and sagging spirits, they departed with better clothes and spirits raised by knowing that someone who cared about their plight was trying to do something about it.

After a time the center began to provide food as well as clothes. This brought in more of what John called his "clients" — skid row residents whom he not only helped, but also talked to so he could understand better what was needed. John in turn broadened and deepened his understanding by living exactly as many of his clients lived.

"Because I wanted to learn what it was really like, learn whether theirs was an acceptable way for people to live," he said, "I stayed in a skid row shelter for eight months. It wasn't great, but I didn't think it was terrible, either. I learned that the shelters served a helpful purpose.

"Later, I lived in a skid row hotel for six months," John continued. "There had been some discussion of tearing down the area's really cheap, cheap housing, like these hotels. I wasn't sure how I felt about that sort of housing, and I thought I should experience it. So I lived in an eight-by-ten-foot room with a sink and public toilet at the end of the hall. Again, I didn't mind it too much, though I knew it wasn't for me."

With this experience plus the knowledge he had gained from hearing problems and concerns voiced by hundreds of skid row residents, John steered the Chrysalis Center into areas beyond clothing and food: into jobs, social service counseling, community organizing, fund raising.

"Dollars weren't the answer to people's problems," he said, "but dollars were necessary to carry on the work.

"I had no real experience, didn't know many people, and wasn't sure where to turn for help. So anytime I was introduced to another new person from outside skid row, I would go to their house or place of business the very next day and convince them that they wanted to help me.

"We started getting good donations — clothes, groceries, volunteer time, some money — and eventually got some top-level people from the Los Angeles business community to serve on the board of directors for the nonprofit organization that was formed around the Chrysalis Center," he said. "I didn't get any pay for the first two and a half years but started receiving a small salary after that for serving as executive director. Basically, I worked up to twenty hours a day, seven days a week."

John estimated that the center's scope of activities became so broad that it eventually provided direct services to some ten thousand people a year, meeting their immediate and long-range needs face-to-face, one on one.

"The masses are important," he noted, "but it's the individual that counts. Thousands of people, one at a time."

In retrospect, it is remarkable to think that none of the thousands who passed through the Chrysalis Center would have received the help they did in the way they did if not for the dedicated work of a solitary young man who lacked money and experience, but not initiative.

"When you see a thing that's wrong, like the conditions on skid row were wrong," John Dillon remarked, "then you should do something to correct it, rather than looking the other way or trying to pass the buck."

For John, the buck stopped on skid row.

Julia Whiley

"I felt that something needed to be done and I was the one who could do it." With those words, Julia Whiley of Clyde, Ohio, was explaining her involvement with a county-sponsored alcohol-rehabilitation program in the nearby town of Fremont, where she had been a schoolteacher for sixteen years.

A fifty-nine-year-old widow and mother

of six children, Julia had no interest in, use for, or knowledge of alcohol rehabilitation until she agreed to provide transportation for a couple who were taking part in one of the programs. Julia would drive them to the counseling and group-therapy sessions, hang around knitting or reading in the rear of the room to kill time, and then drive them home.

After a number of visits, though, she found herself "getting hooked" by a common theme being repeated in various ways by participants in the sessions. Julia heard those involved, many of them high school dropouts, lament time and again their lack of basic education skills such as reading and math. The story they told usually went like this: "If I had more education, I could get a high school diploma, and with that I could get a job, or a better job." Implied but seldom voiced was the progression from inadequate schooling, to a poor job, to low self-esteem, to alcohol abuse.

"These people needed help," Julia observed. "They needed somebody to step in and do something about their lack of education. Why not me?" Why not, indeed. Julia had been a teacher for twenty years, most of that time spent teaching remedial reading.

With enthusiastic encouragement from those running the program, Julia began donating her time and expertise twice a week as a tutor, instructing recovering alcoholics one-to-one on basic math and English, as well as the finer points of how to pass the test that would qualify them for high school equivalency diplomas.

Julia's initiative never changed the world, but it changed some lives. And that made it worth her considerable effort. "I always felt if you were able to help just one other person have a little better life," she said, "then you had succeeded." Julia Whiley did not fail.

Clive and Kelly Edmunds

Without initiative, Clive and Kelly Edmunds would have been just two more faces in the crowd, two more bystanders huddled together, watching and whispering at the scene of a fatal one-car accident late at night on New Jersey's Garden State Parkway. Without initiative, the couple from Villas, New Jersey, would have waited with the others for the arrival of police and firemen to remove the body of a young woman from the front seat of the crumpled, smoldering automobile on the roadside. Without initiative, the Edmundses later would have joined the others in grieving because they had stood by while an infant, hidden by debris in the backseat of the wrecked car, died a slow, suffocating death. Thankfully, Clive and Kelly were not without initiative.

"We were driving home a little after 2:30 A.M. when we saw some sort of accident. Just in case we might be able to do something, we stopped," said Clive, thirty-two, a sports car mechanic. "There were already people standing around, but Kelly's a nurse, so we thought she could help.

"I asked the people who were standing some little distance from this wrecked car if anyone had checked to see exactly what the situation was, and they said they had looked and seen a woman dead in the front seat," he continued. "I questioned whether there was anyone else in the car, and they said they didn't think so. They hadn't seen anyone else, and now they didn't want to get too close because there was a fire underneath the engine and they were concerned that the wreck might explode or something.

"Being a mechanic," Clive went on, "I knew there wasn't too much immediate danger, so I took a chance and ran over to the car to see if the others had missed anything. Kelly was right behind me.

"The automobile was utterly destroyed. It had hit a tree at high speed," he said. "Doors were ripped off, windows were shattered, and everything was a jumble inside. We could see the woman sprawled across the front seat. Kelly checked on her."

Mrs. Edmunds, twenty-seven, carefully examined the crash victim for signs of life. "But there was nothing," she said, "no vital signs at all. She was completely gone."

Having confirmed that unhappy fact, the couple turned their attention to the rest of the car, or what remained of it. On first glance, it appeared that those who had arrived ahead of them were correct in presuming that the woman was alone in the auto, for all was silent — deathly silent — within the tangled debris. As Clive looked more closely, however, his gaze was arrested by something in the backseat.

"There had been such an impact that the doors were folded right in and the top was pushed down," he recounted. "Even so, I caught sight of what looked like the top of a child's car-seat safety harness. We've got harnesses like those for our two little boys, so I thought it looked familiar. I decided to look underneath the door panel that was covering it."

Clive's voice grew tense as he continued his narrative.

"When I forced back the panel slightly and peeked in, I was surprised to see a child underneath there," he said. "And I was shocked — no, amazed — when I saw her move a little. She was alive! But her head and neck had been forced sideways at about a ninety-degree angle, clear all the way over. She was trying to breathe, but couldn't, and obviously couldn't make any sort of sound. As soon as I ripped the door panel away, her neck straightened up and she started screaming.

"Kelly told me, 'That's good! That's a good sign. If she's screaming, she's responsive. Keep her in the safety seat and let's get her to the hospital fast,'" Clive said, recalling those breathlessly hectic moments.

"There were no police cars or ambulances on the scene yet, so I just seized the initiative and took the child to our car," he explained. "The hospital wasn't far away, and I knew right where it was because that's where our younger son had been delivered nine months earlier. That made him the same age as this little girl we just pulled out of the wreck."

Telling bystanders to inform the police when they arrived that the Edmundses were driving her to the hospital, Clive and Kelly piled into their car and hurried the child to the emergency room.

Doctors there determined that the infant had suffered a fractured skull, a broken leg, severe cuts, and other injuries. Nevertheless, they said, because she had received medical attention so promptly, she would recover completely from the crash that killed her mother. Clearly, said the doctors, Clive and Kelly had spared the baby's life.

"Her family phoned to thank us, and their friends did the same, thanking us for what we did. That was all very nice, but we found ourselves embarrassed," remarked Clive. "I mean, it's embarrassing to be thanked for saving a baby. Who wouldn't want to save a baby?

"I guess it was just that we did something the others who were there didn't do," he said. "Some of the people at the scene said they were afraid they could be sued if they did anything, or that they might get in trouble for tampering with evidence in a fatal accident. But that didn't seem right. Obviously, if police or ambulance people had been there, we would have let them take the lead. But they were nowhere in sight. We felt it was our responsibility to show the way. The situation needed somebody to take hold of it."

Clive and Kelly Edmunds did take hold. With bold initiative, they wrested a baby girl's life from the grip of death.

Raul Natividad

Raul Natividad shows turkey and trimmings he'll deliver to sixteen families for Thanksgiving. (Photo by Luis Villalobos/El Paso Times.)

"People who think that one individual on his own can't make a difference are a hundred percent wrong," said Raul Natividad. "It's amazing what one person can do to make things better, if you just put your mind to it. All you have to do is sit down, look at what's going on around you, and ask yourself, *What needs to be done?* Then you go out and you do it."

That was a simple recipe, but it was one that worked well for Raul, sixty-four, as he toiled quietly year after year to improve the lot of impoverished families around his El Paso, Texas, community.

A retired postal worker with six grown children and eight grandchildren, Raul began his activities while still raising a family and working full-time. In fact, it was on his job as a letter carrier that Raul first recognized conditions about which he as an individual felt he could do something.

"I delivered mail in some of the poorer areas of El Paso. I saw a lot of families that were really hard up," he said. "I mentioned it to one of the ladies at church, and we talked about what I could do to help." They concluded that the surest answer was food.

"I started out by helping a few families with food packages at Christmas," he recalled. "The next year, I did the same again but expanded it to cover Thanksgiving as well. Eventually, because so many big charities took care of Christmas, I concentrated on Thanksgiving."

Raul explained how he worked. "Five or six weeks before the holiday, I would buy a couple of turkeys or hams and go to a ball game or some other public place and raffle them off," he said. "With the profits from these, I'd buy a few more and raffle those off, too. And so on. After a while, between the raffles and donations that people made, there would be enough for me to start buying.

"Not just holiday food, although I always included a turkey and other traditional stuff," Raul pointed out. "I wanted to do more than give them one meal. So I included staple items like ten or twenty pounds of pinto beans, some flour, even cold cereal. I dealt with a market that gave a volume discount, which made the money go farther. All of my gasoline and similar expenses came out of my own pocket so that every penny of every dollar raised went to the poor."

As Thanksgiving drew near, Raul and his relatives, along with other volunteers, would neatly box their bounty for each individual family and then deliver it a day or two before the holiday.

"I always made sure to limit my efforts to a size that was manageable," he said. "The first year something like twenty families were involved, and by last year — the twelfth in a row, I think — it had grown to forty. But I could still handle it without any slipups.

"And I could keep track of these families during the year to see what their needs were, in case there was some other help I could send their way," he noted. "Keep your eyes open, and you can always come up with a pair of kid's shoes, a set of crutches, a bed, a screen door, a stove, whatever. It's a never-ending process. People always have needs."

With individual initiative, Raul Natividad went a long way to meet them.

David Martz

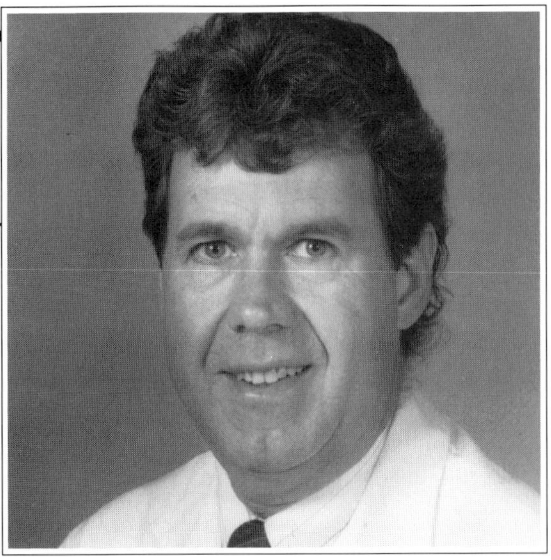

In the glorious footrace, the great discovery, or the historic breakthrough, the last step is always remembered; the first one is usually forgotten. Yet there can be no final step until that first step — that difficult act of initiative — has been taken.

It was with considerable difficulty that Dr. David Martz of Colorado Springs, Colorado, took the first short step on what became the road to long life for a man whose survival had been measured in months.

David, forty-two, was an internist specializing in tumor and blood disorders when he accepted an invitation to join a group of about thirty college students traveling to the Central American country of Honduras for several weeks of mobile health clinic work.

Arriving in Honduras, the team visited numerous remote villages, examining and treating about one hundred people a day for a wide range of medical complaints. It was near the end of this tour that Dr. Martz diagnosed an ailment he could not treat. The case involved a twenty-nine-year-old man who had such a serious cardiac condition that each time his heart would beat, the resounding pressure caused his head to wobble. David recognized that this was a job for specialists, surgeons who could replace a faulty valve in the man's heart.

Without the operation, the American doctor knew this patient had only a few months to live, a year at the outside. So Dr. Martz put his diagnosis into a letter that the man could take to Honduran health authorities in order to get proper treatment.

Having completed his volunteer work, David then returned home to Colorado, where several months later he received an unexpected communication. A Honduran health worker wrote to inform Dr. Martz that the young man with the bad heart (his name was Adolfo) had after long delay undergone open-heart surgery, only to be told by local doctors that his condition was beyond their ability to repair. She related that they had closed up his chest and sent him home to die. Then she asked David, "Is there anything that you can do?"

"My first response," he recalled, "was to ask, 'What kind of magician does she think I am?' I was frustrated and almost angry that I was being asked to do more than I had already done. I couldn't perform the surgery myself, and I despaired of getting anyone with that level of surgical skill to travel to Honduras. So what else was there? I stewed over this for a couple of weeks and got nowhere," said Dr. Martz. "But slowly, I became less resistant to the whole idea. I thought to myself, *If this were a relative of mine, would I do more than I'm doing now?* Of course the answer was yes. I would find a way, somehow.

"Then it occurred to me that if I couldn't get the help to Adolfo, maybe I could get Adolfo to the help — that is, bring him here for treatment. But again, I was reluctant because there wasn't any money for this and everything would have to be donated," David said. "Frankly, I had to overcome the fear of being rejected, of seeming silly or ridiculous in the eyes of my medical colleagues for even making such a suggestion. However, I told myself that being rejected should be a trivial matter for someone like me who had gone through medical school and raised a family and all of that. After all, a man's life was at stake."

"One person can make a difference."

Overcoming his own uncertainty represented the first difficult step for Dr. Martz. The steps that followed came far more easily.

"I phoned a local cardiologist friend of mine, Dr. Robert Cadigan," said David. "He readily agreed to donate his diagnostic services and suggested I ask Dr. Claude Oliver to do the actual surgery. Dr. Oliver said he would be pleased to. Once people started saying yes, it wasn't so tough." With Drs. Cadigan and Oliver in place, David quickly lined up a full surgical team, persuaded a local hospital to donate its facilities, and enlisted the aid of the First United Methodist Church of Colorado Springs in financing Adolfo's travel expenses.

Adolfo spent his thirtieth birthday in a Colorado Springs hospital, recovering from successful surgery that gave him a strong, normal heart and the prospect of a long, normal life.

The operation also gave something to David Martz: an insight into individual initiative. "One person *can* make a difference," he said. "But not if you don't try. Things happen only when you take that first step."

Naomi Rice

It was 3:00 A.M., and Naomi Rice found herself suddenly, unexpectedly wide awake. In the predawn solitude, her mind was positively racing. "I had a complete plan in my head, every detail!" she remembered. "I knew exactly what I was going to do." She crept out of bed and began writing it all down.

The words that Naomi recorded were the basis for a remarkable initiative that grew over many years to become a source of pride for a large retirement community and a source of relief for thousands of residents there who thought they had nowhere to turn.

When Naomi and her husband, John, moved to Crestwood, a collection of senior citizen villages near Lakehurst, New Jersey, there were only about a thousand residents. But already problems were cropping up for people coming to grips with the many difficulties of retirement and aging: financial constraints, loneliness, declining health.

"I got interested in this as a Welcome Wagon hostess when I started seeing some things that worried me," Naomi explained. "Mostly, it was people's needs not being met. We were kind of isolated, and it seemed that there was no one to help with these things, nobody to care.

"In my heart I knew I wanted to do something, but I had doubts. I kept asking myself, *What can I do? What can one person accomplish?* Then I woke up at three that morning with the idea for Somebody Cares," she said.

Naomi conceived of Somebody Cares as a community self-help program permitting resident volunteers to fulfill the needs of their neighbors. It would be supported entirely by donations, and no one would be compensated.

Mrs. Rice, who had some business training in her background, started by enlisting the backing of the community developer, who set up Somebody Cares with free office space, utilities, and the like for the first several years of its existence. Next, she rounded up volunteers and began raising financial support "on faith — faith that we could achieve something."

In the early stages, Somebody Cares concentrated on basic needs like Meals on Wheels and rudimentary transportation services.

But as the community expanded, eventually reaching 17,000 residents, things grew more sophisticated in order to keep pace with requirements.

"We built a Somebody Cares headquarters building and organized a system of daily phone calls to keep track of shut-ins," said Naomi, who described her age as "seventy-three going on twenty-eight." "We purchased some station wagons and signed up volunteer drivers to provide regular, free transportation to anyone in the community. Later, we got more station wagons and a van equipped with a wheelchair lift. We set up a plan for loaning equipment such as hospital beds. Then we got into counseling, social referrals, and a whole range of services."

After thirteen years, Somebody Cares was able to boast more than 350 regular volunteers on its rolls, responding to over 23,000 requests for assistance in a single year.

"It's remarkable what this one woman has done to help," commented Thomas Devon, a Crestwood neighbor of Naomi's. "Before her, so many people had so many problems, but nowhere to turn."

Thanks to the vision and initiative of Naomi Rice, they found somewhere to turn.

The Gaskinses

If seeing a need and meeting it through your own resources is what initiative is all about, then Mary Ann and Henry Gaskins of Washington, D.C., were a study in the meaning of that word.

The Gaskinses were well situated in satisfying careers — he as a supervisory librarian in the Library of Congress and she as an administrative consultant to NASA — when they recognized a desperate need for more emphasis on education among blacks. Henry and Mary Ann, themselves black, had been highly successful in motivating their own five children toward a quest for learning and higher education. But the couple often found similar drive lacking in the black community at large.

"There's simply not enough stress put on education in the black community," Mrs. Gaskins, forty-six, observed. "Far too many black youngsters harbor visions of becoming overnight superstars in sports or entertainment, without realizing that the chances of this happening are one in a million or less."

Having seen the need, the Gaskinses responded to it. Henry, fifty-two, with a doctorate in education, had held a part-time job for a number of years with a tutoring service that catered to the educational aspirations of advantaged young people who were sharpening their skills in order to reach topflight universities.

"For a fee of thirty-five dollars an hour," he said, "these kids were being prepared for scholarships at some of the best schools in the country. But my wife and I knew that most black families couldn't afford this, so we decided to make it available free of charge."

The product of the couple's decision became the Freedom Youth Academy, a kind of school away from school that the

Gaskinses established in their comfortable southeast Washington home.

Every weekday evening from four to eight and all day Saturdays, Mr. and Mrs. Gaskins (he with the boys upstairs and she with the girls downstairs) would provide minority children with one-to-one tutoring in basic learning skills, educational enrichment, college preparation, and motivation. They employed the latest techniques and hardware, including videocassette lessons and computer terminals. They tutored as many as seventy-five youngsters a week, for several years footing the entire expense themselves. But after Henry gave up his part-time job in order to devote more attention to the academy, he and Mary Ann began asking those who could afford it to contribute five dollars a week toward the cost of books, supplies, software, equipment, and the like. Despite that, the venture remained a big financial loser.

But it was a bigger educational winner. Over the course of a decade, the Gaskinses nurtured and developed close to four hundred disadvantaged children — some simply mastering school fundamentals, but others honing their skills with higher education in mind. Of the many high school seniors who attended and stuck with the tutoring, 98 percent went on to college or university, more than a few of them on scholarship.

"There's a great need for this kind of help, and that's what motivates us to stay with it," remarked Henry. "We put a lot into it, but we get a lot out, too. It's tremendously satisfying to see these children progress and make something of themselves."

The Gaskinses saw a need and through their own initiative filled it. By opening the door to their home, Henry and Mary Ann opened the door to opportunity for disadvantaged youngsters by the hundreds.

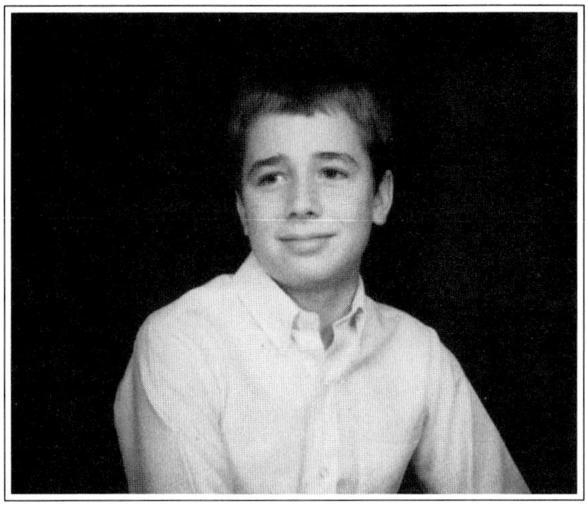

Nathan Tolbert

To understand the gravity of things, it was necessary only to glance at Angi Howell's throat. The girl's self-inflicted claw marks bore terrifying witness to the frenzy that had seized her as she nearly choked to death. Her survival bore inspiring witness to the initiative of Nathan Tolbert.

Ten-year-old Nathan of White Hall, Arkansas, was returning home from a Boy Scout outing when he stopped for a drink of water at the Peace Tabernacle Church of White Hall, where Angi's father was pastor.

It being a Saturday, the church was nearly deserted. Angi herself probably would have been off playing somewhere if she hadn't been preparing to take her weekly lesson from a piano teacher who at that moment was working with another student. As Angi waited in the hallway outside the piano room, she popped a peppermint sweet into her mouth.

That might have been the last act of her life if it hadn't been for Nathan, who entered the hallway from outdoors a few moments later. Glancing down the corridor, he noticed Angi at the other end and voiced a greeting. But the girl, who was a year or two older than Nathan, did not reply. She could not. The piece of hard candy had become lodged in her throat, blocking her windpipe and sending her into a panicked, futile effort to save herself.

"Angi was turning white and grabbing at her throat, trying to get the candy out," said Nathan. Rushing toward her, he saw that in her desperation she was actually tearing at her throat with her fingers.

"Sometimes, fairy tales happen...."

"I just automatically turned her around and did what the Scouts taught me," recalled Nathan. A couple of years earlier, in Cub Scouts, he had learned first aid including the Heimlich maneuver. "I wrapped my arms around where her rib cage ends and yanked real hard," he said. The procedure compressed her lungs, forced residual air upward, expelled the candy, and restored the breath of life to a grateful Angi.

The girl said that while there had been other people nearby, they weren't aware of her distress because she couldn't make the slightest sound to alert them. "So it really was all up to Nathan to save me," she said.

"What really got everybody's attention," observed Nathan's father, Stanley Tolbert, "was the responsibility and initiative that a boy of ten showed in rescuing Angi himself, instead of wasting time looking for someone else to do it. Of course, for me there was nothing new in that, because Nathan's always been a take-charge type of kid," Stanley went on. "He wants to be the leader in anything he does. He doesn't need any prompting. Show him something one time, and you never have to show him again."

Nathan's lifesaving exploit brought him more than a dozen commendations along with a good deal of publicity, which Stanley said the boy handled well, given that it came at an especially sad and difficult time. Only a few weeks earlier Nathan's mother had died following the birth of his little sister.

But in a happy postscript to the story, those two events — Nathan's saving one life after losing another — were joined by a coincidence that was recounted by the boy's father.

"The instructor who taught Nathan the Heimlich maneuver in the Cub Scouts was a nurse named Sandy Jones," said Stanley. "We all went to the same church together, and Nathan was real close to Sandy. He liked her a lot.

"Well, after my wife passed away, I also got to know Sandy, and I liked her, too. Things moved on from there, and we got married. So now Nathan and my little daughter have a new Mommy. I guess that sounds kind of like a fairy tale, doesn't it?" he asked.

"Well, sometimes fairy tales happen," someone answered.

Stanley said, "I believe it."

AMERICANS AT PLAY

The dynamic principle of fantasy
is play, which belongs also
to the child,
and as such it appears to be
inconsistent with the principle
of serious work.
But without this playing
with fantasy
no creative work has ever yet
come to birth. The debt we owe
to the play of imagination
is incalculable.

CARL GUSTAV JUNG

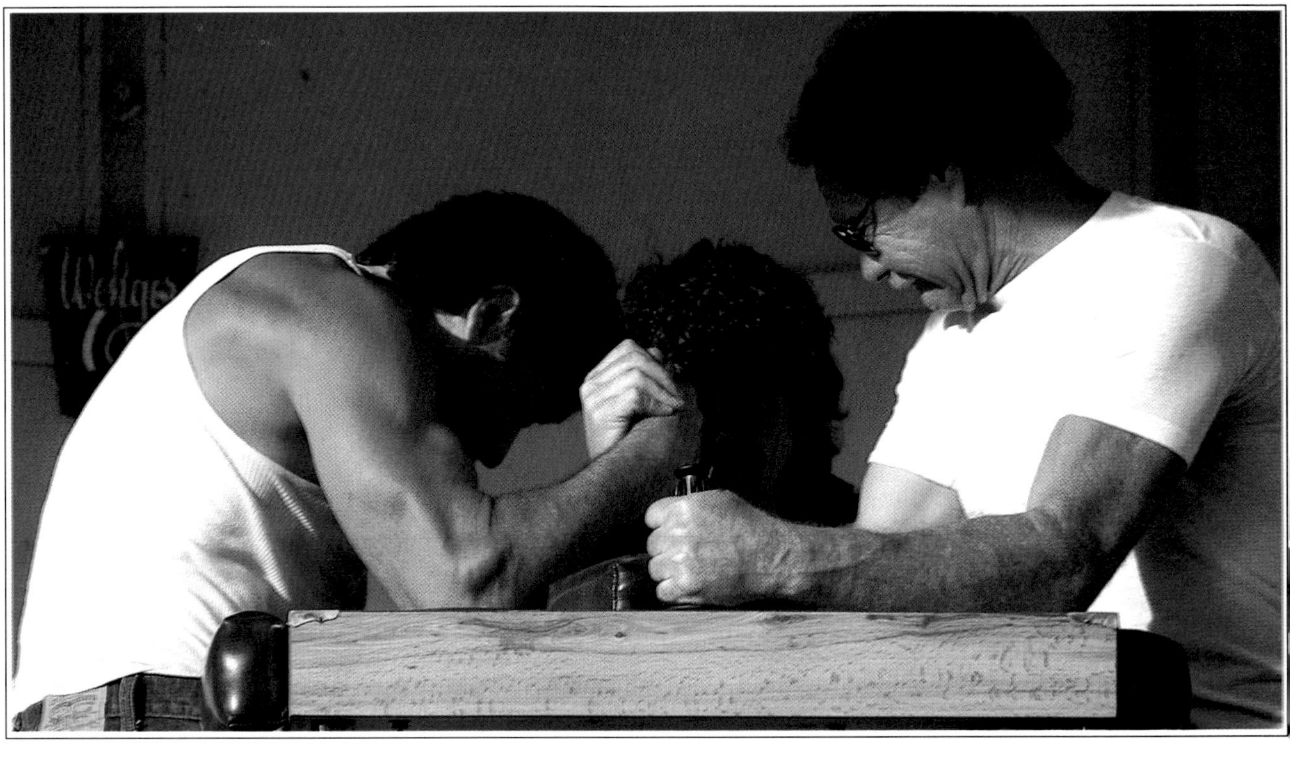

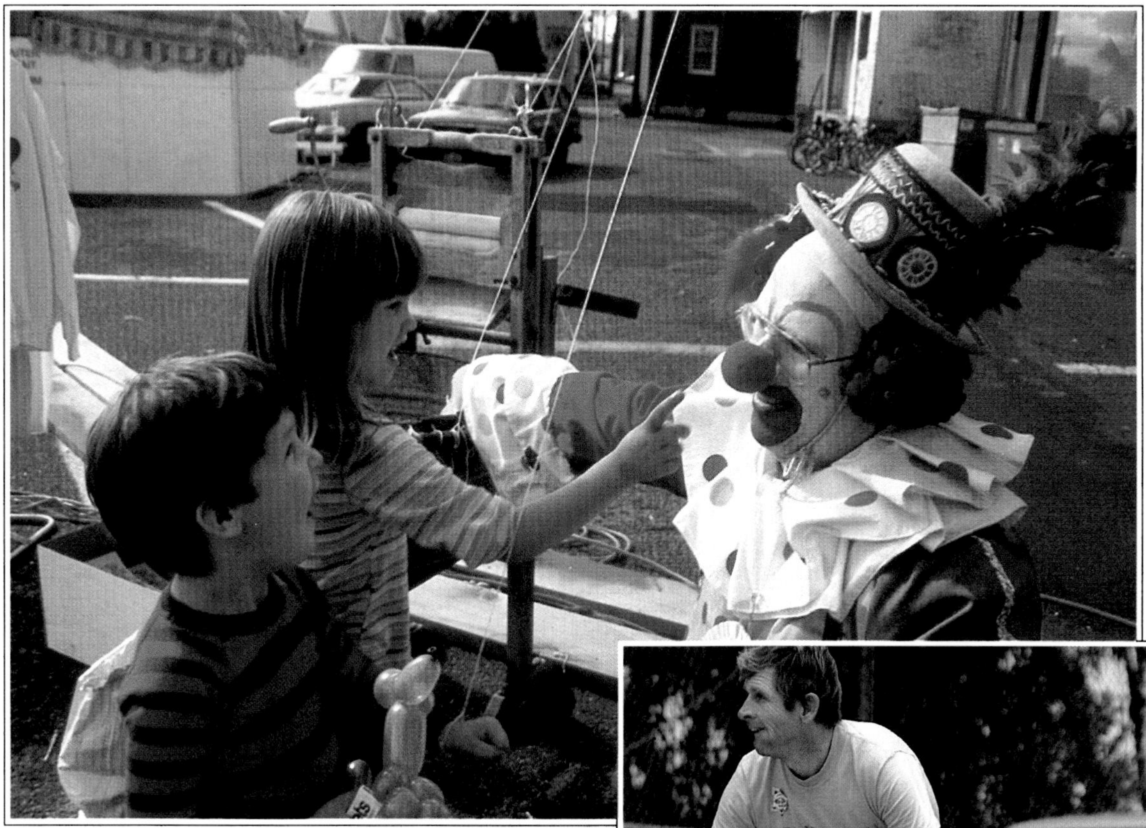

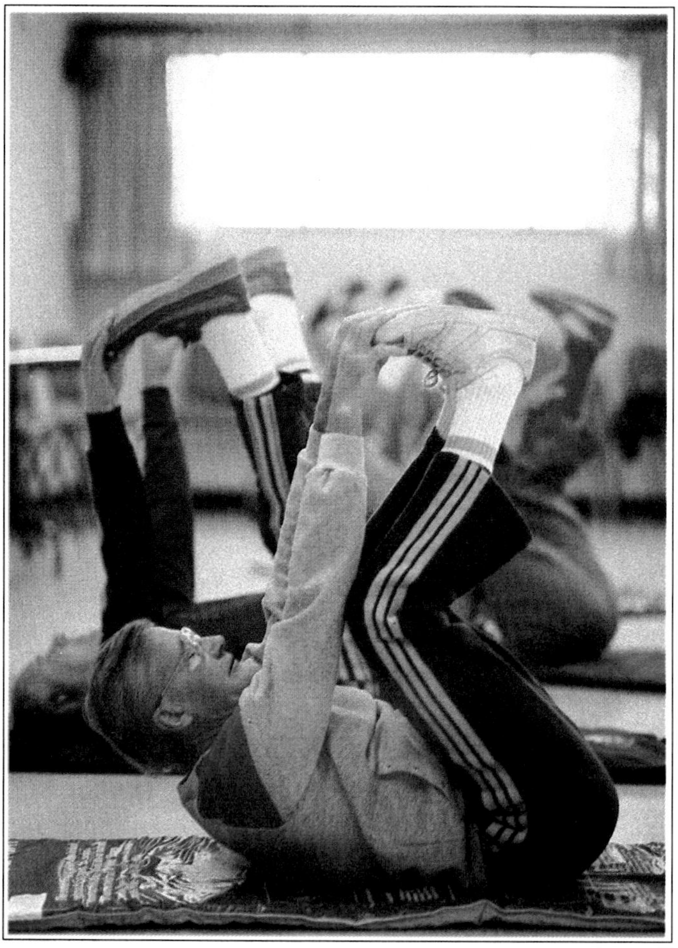

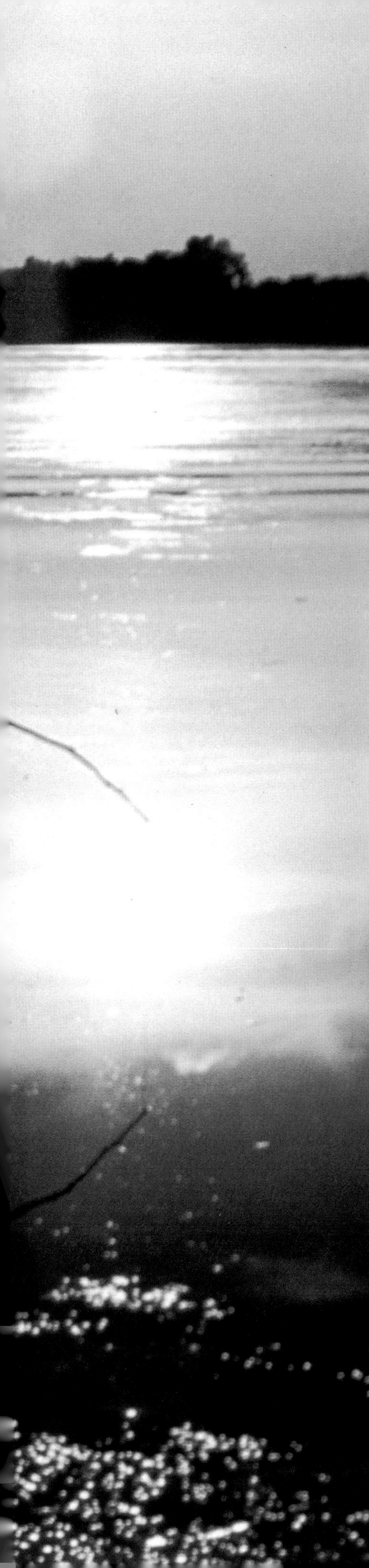

CAL AGGIES

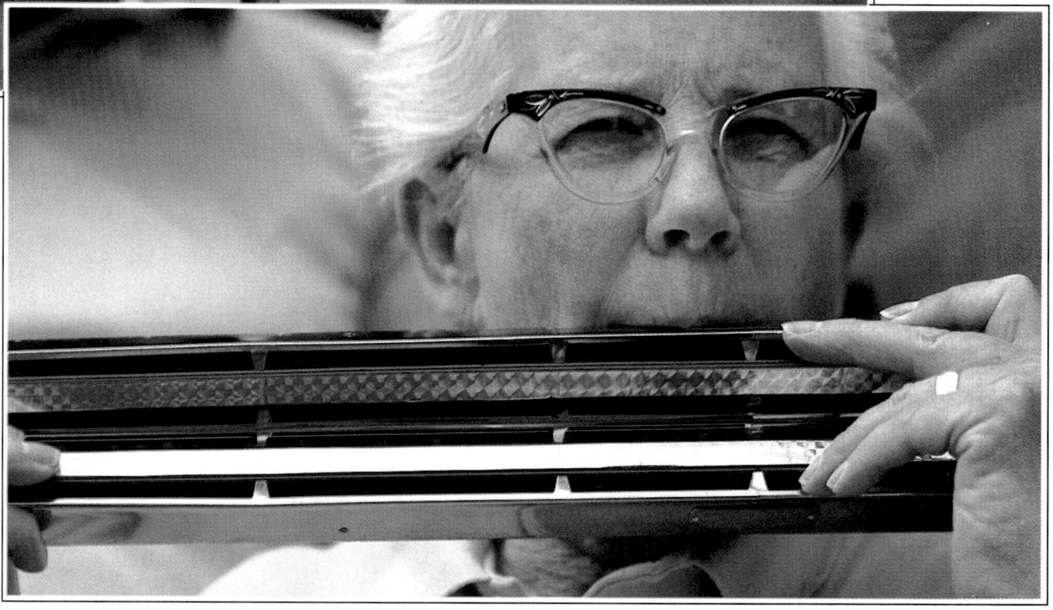

ICATED TO THE
SERVATION OF JAZZ

38

PERSEVERANCE

Between achievement and disappointment, the difference as often as not is perseverance: The determination to hang on and press ahead in the face of adversity. Americans are an achieving people; they persevere.

The sturdy fiber of grit and resolve that is perseverance was woven into the fabric of American life from the beginning, starting with the first settlers. Those bold newcomers braved deprivation, isolation, and death. Indeed, more than half of the Plymouth colonists died during their first winter in America. Yet the survivors stuck with their mission; they persevered, as did those who followed in their footsteps.

Americans from the *Mayflower* to the moon landing and beyond have never shrunk from hardships; they have challenged them, taken them in stride, and gloried in overcoming them. They have confronted problems both public and private with an optimistic attitude of mind which understands that the only way to guarantee failure is to give up, while the only hope of success is to try.

Along the way, Americans have fostered a distinctive brand of perseverance that encourages people not simply to survive troubles, but to prevail over them and excel despite them.

Perseverance in the American character represents both the courage to endure what is immutable and the will to change what is not.

Betsey and Barbara

Barbara Lombardi (sitting) and Betsey Lombardi Doane operating their radio station.

Two individuals of uncommon perseverance and achievement were Betsey Doane and Barbara Lombardi of Shelton, Connecticut.

Twin sisters in their early forties, Betsey and Barbara shared many things beyond an obvious similarity of features. Both enjoyed high-level careers: Betsey as a professor of mathematics and computer science at Housatonic Community College, and Barbara as clinical coordinator and acting director of the Lower Naugatuck Valley Council on Drug and Alcohol Abuse. The pair excelled academically, each holding not one but two master's degrees — Barbara's in history and counseling, Betsey's in math and computer sciences. Both sisters were licensed "ham" radio operators frequently involved with the American Radio Relay League in its worldwide emergency communications network during earthquakes, hurricanes, and similar calamities. The two women regularly volunteered with the American Red Cross, and both made music an important part of life — Betsey as a pianist and church organist, and Barbara as an avid audiophile.

Even as the sisters shared their satisfactions over what they had done and could do, so they shared their frustrations over what they had not done and could not do. Neither could drive a car or play a game of tennis. Neither could read a newspaper or view a TV soap opera. Neither could watch a sunrise or spot a hawk on the wing.

Neither could see.

Both were blind at birth and went through life unable to distinguish anything with their eyes except light and dark.

Yet while Barbara and Betsey had limited vision, they came to realize that they had unlimited potential, which was something their family stressed at every opportunity.

"As far back as I can remember," said Barbara, "nobody close to us said we couldn't do things. They always told us we could. We were brought up to understand that we would have to work for a living, would have to do something with our lives, and that this was a task we'd have to achieve for ourselves."

The barriers of blindness notwithstanding, the girls began achieving early in life.

Betsey took up music at the age of five, studying piano and organ while Barbara served as critic, exhorting her sister, "Don't play it *that* way, play it *this* way," and then humming for her twin how she thought the passage should be rendered. As they grew to adulthood, their musical interests diverged, with Barbara delving into hi-fi equipment to indulge an eclectic musical interest, while Betsey continued classical studies and played the organ on Sundays at St. Lawrence Roman Catholic Church in nearby Huntington.

Then there was radio. Coached by an uncle, the precocious, unseeing twins mastered the complexities of shortwave radio while not yet even in their teens, passing numerous required tests to earn their amateur radio licenses at the age of twelve. More than a quarter of a century later, they were still flicking switches, adjusting dials, tuning in on and talking to the world.

It was over ham radio that Betsey first met Paul Doane, whom she later married.

Afterward, whenever an American Radio Relay League emergency might arise, Paul, Betsey, and Barbara would gather in the radio room of the Doanes' house and work — sometimes nonstop for days on end — at getting messages into and out of the world's disaster areas.

Anytime there was a need, the sisters would be found donating their services to the Red Cross, usually arranging emergency home leaves for military personnel.

"What with teaching, studying, running a household, keeping up with ham operations, volunteering, and practicing music, I sometimes don't know how everything gets done," Betsey remarked at the end of one particularly trying day. "It does get a little hectic now and then," she added with a matter-of-factness that made it evident she considered her life and work entirely unremarkable.

She was joined in this by Barbara, who voiced the opinion that she and Betsey were no different from other folks except for lacking vision. "Don't get me wrong; that's an important limitation," said Barbara, "but *everybody* has limitations — you, me, everyone. There are things Betsey and I can't do that other people can do. But there probably are things we can do that they can't."

Betsey, for example, delighted in recounting the deceptive ease with which Barbara, wearing headphones, could carry on a face-to-face conversation with two or three people while at the same time transmitting and receiving shortwave radio messages in the "beep ... beep-beep ... beeeep" language of Morse code.

"Certainly, our limitations are not the same as those of most people," said Barbara, "but we all have limits, and we all get frustrated with them and have to deal with them. In our case, family, friends, and teachers helped us to cope by giving encouragement," she continued. "When people boost your self-image and don't discourage you from doing something but continually encourage you, you're more apt to have the determination to do it. We always heard the same message: Try your hardest, do your best.

A lunch-pail approach to success.

"We learned to become adaptable, to find alternate methods of doing things. Anytime somebody suggested that we couldn't do this or that because we were blind, we only half-listened, because the other half would be busy figuring out ways to adapt so that we could do it."

When someone asked Betsey how she might explain the success that she and Barbara achieved, Mrs. Doane pointed without hesitation to the sisters' lunch-pail philosophy of life: "You get up every day and you go to your job and you do all that you can do, and then you go back the next day and you do the same again."

"That's right," Barbara chipped in, "you work at it. You don't give up. Another thing: You get over being afraid. Don't be afraid to try, and don't be afraid to fail, because you learn by your failures and you grow with them," she said.

"Above all, remember that you can't lose by trying. The only way to achieve is to try and never stop trying."

What Barbara Lombardi and Betsey Doane described in their own way was an attitude: The triumphant attitude of perseverance that had lifted a veil of darkness for two little blind girls and lighted their path with the brilliant promise of human potential, which is the light that never fails.

Don Baerman

Don Baerman demonstrating that he has "no handicap" on the golf course. (Daytona Beach News Journal photo by Michael Takash.)

When the One Great Scorer comes
to write against your name,
He marks not that you won or lost,
but how you played the game

Grantland Rice

To Don Baerman of Daytona Beach, Florida, those words by an immortal sports writer symbolized more than motivation, more than inspiration. They represented a philosophy, an attitude, an entire way of life for Don, who liked Rice's memorable verse better with one word changed.

"It's not so much *how* you play the game," he said, "but *that* you play the game — some game, any game."

Don's game was golf. He loved it, never tired of it, had been at it for almost sixty years, starting as a caddy in Hamilton, Ohio, when he was just nine years old.

At present, he was regaling a listener with details of a recent triumph — every golfer's pride and joy, a hole in one.

"It happened in a tournament at Pelican Bay," he related, alluding to the Daytona Beach country club where he was a member and did most of his golfing. "The hole was a 160-yard par three, and I aced it with a five wood," he said, satisfaction bubbling in his voice.

"I had another hole in one, even longer, in 1979," he added. That was when Don, a retired accountant, and Aggie, his wife of more than forty years, still lived in Ohio. "On that occasion," he said, "the hole was 193 yards, and I used a four wood. From the tee, it looked like my ball had rolled past the hole. But when I got to the green, there it was, in the bottom of the cup!"

Those were the only holes in one of Don's long career, but they more than satisfied him. After all, some folks golfed a lifetime and got none, even playing on two good legs.

Don accomplished his on one.

A surgeon had given him the grim news back in 1956: One of his legs was being amputated because of complications from childhood osteomyelitis. It was his right leg, and he was right-handed. When Don asked how this would affect his golfing, the doctor answered him straight: "You've played your last game," he said.

"That put drive in me, challenged me," Don recalled. "When I heard that, I was determined to play again."

But determination collided with reality when Don learned that, because the leg was removed so near his hip, he couldn't be fitted with an artificial limb that allowed him to move comfortably. "Too many straps and buckles," he said.

Unable to find a suitable prosthesis, it appeared that Don may indeed have shot his last round of golf, just as the surgeon had forecast.

Still, the dedicated golfer wasn't inclined to give up without a struggle. He was only in his mid-thirties, had always been active, and knew that other leg-amputees had played successfully. *If they can do it, I can do it,* he remembered telling himself.

"I said to heck with the artificial leg and started working without it."

Less than four months after the amputation, Don — balanced on one leg — was playing himself back into shape by taking a carton of golf balls to the edge of a mowed cornfield and whacking them as far as he could with a driver, then paying neighborhood kids a penny apiece to retrieve them.

"Aggie's part in all of this was crucial," Don said. "She'd never been a golfer, wasn't much interested in the game, and often was a golf widow. But she really helped when it counted. She was so supportive. Patient, too."

Don also had to be patient. He knew his game would never again be what it had been, which was pretty good. He'd previously played to a four handicap, meaning that he was nearly a "scratch" golfer — able to compete on even terms, without a scoring advantage. But now, following the amputation, who knew how high his handicap would go? Probably into double figures.

Yet with practice and perseverance Don improved, discovering that he could drive and putt quite well using his one-legged stance, could make his way around most courses with a golf cart, and could play out of sand traps and roughs by steadying himself on crutches.

With a positive outlook, he even perceived some benefit in his crippling impairment.

"Since I now was on one leg instead of two, I couldn't shift weight on my drives," he explained. "This made it easier to control my head movement, and not moving your head on drives is rule number one in golf."

Before much time had passed, Don found himself involved in organized amputee golf activities, which gave him the perspective to appreciate that while he had his troubles, other people had theirs, too — some more severe than his own.

"I saw competitors with two artificial legs, others with no hands or arms wearing double hooks," he recalled. "But they were still playing, and pretty well, at that."

Don went on to serve as president of the National Amputee Golf Association and, with Aggie's encouragement, to play in as many amputee tournaments as he could manage all around the country.

Those contests were important, Don said, because they were where the public, including people demoralized by their own disabilities, got to see amputees capably at play, enjoying themselves.

"What matters isn't what you *don't* have,

but what you *do* have," Don said. "You've got to take whatever that is and use it. Not necessarily golfing. But doing something. Doing anything.

"The message that needs to reach people with impairments is not that we amputees are so great, but that we're out there participating," he said, punctuating his point with the pendulum swing of an imaginary putter. "Even when I'm playing bad, I'm still playing, and that's good."

Before he lost his leg, Don Baerman had proven himself a four-handicap player in the game of golf. After that, he proved himself a scratch player in the game of life.

Roy Siegel

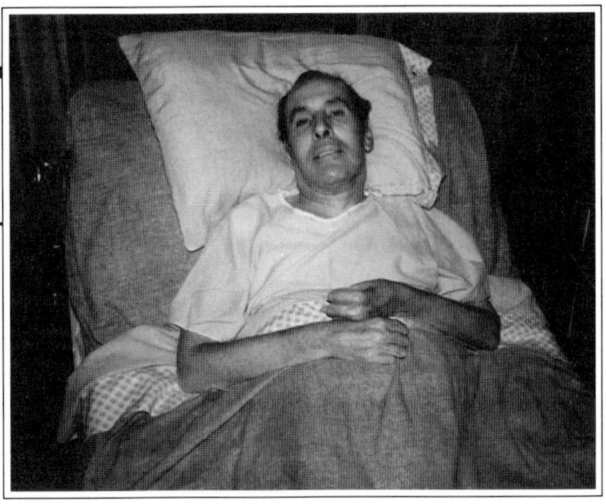

To face grim fortune with good cheer demands a singular spirit, the unquenchable spirit of a man like Roy Siegel.

Roy was an Easton, Pennsylvania, resident who had everything to live for — wife, children, home, career — when calamity struck and crippled the very capacities that many people consider essential for life: independence, self-sufficiency, mobility.

Starting in his late forties, Roy experienced increasing weakness, gradually losing his ability to walk, then to stand, then to sit, eventually even to move. By his mid-fifties, Roy was a quadriplegic, paralyzed from the neck down: an intellect and personality imprisoned in a body unlikely to ever function again, although it would live a long time. The multiple sclerosis that enfeebled him wasn't terminal, it was simply interminable — chronic, progressive, and irreversible in its damaging effects on the central nervous system.

With the future holding only a bedridden, invalid existence, Roy might have despaired of life and withdrawn, angry and bitter over the ill fate that had laid him low. Astonishingly, quite the opposite happened: Roy embraced life, symbolically reaching out to touch troubled people with his optimism and cheerful disposition.

"There was no point in me lying there feeling sorry for myself," he explained to a caller who chatted with Roy over a speakerphone beside the hospital-style bed that he occupied in the downstairs of his home.

"So I said to myself, *Seeing that I'm crippled and there's nothing I can do to help me, maybe there's something I can do to help others.*"

But what? How could a man unable to move, permanently confined to bed, possibly help anyone else?

Roy found his answer in thoughtful reflection.

"From the standpoint of thinking," he remarked, "this multiple sclerosis was really a blessing in disguise. Because when you're flat on your back with nowhere to go, you can do an awful lot of thinking and put things in their proper perspective."

Part of the perspective Roy developed

showed him that despite his paralysis, he was not helpless; he was not without resources. He saw that he still had his faith, his intelligence, his voice, his keen sense of humor. These tools he put to work in the service of others.

What he contrived was something he called "The 25th Hour," a monthly series of audiotape cassettes containing amusing stories, jokes, and observations on one side, and a variety of musical numbers — mostly show tunes — on the other. Assisted by his wife, Terry, his four grown children, and his nurse, Roy organized his material, got it recorded onto a master cassette, and had it duplicated, one painstaking copy at a time. The cassettes then were distributed free of charge to nursing home residents, shut-ins, and the bereaved, reaching locations as near as his own community and as distant as Europe.

Roy worked at his project for many years, mailing out thousands of cassettes at the rate of eighty copies a month. He covered his expenses with help from a financial angel called "Aunt Esther," who sent him monthly support of one hundred dollars.

"What I'm doing with 'The 25th Hour' is trying to cheer people up by getting their minds off themselves — off their problems, their losses, their health, whatever," Roy said.

"This makes me very happy because I'm helping other people and *accomplishing* something."

Under the circumstances, the things that Roy accomplished may have surprised some people, but he was not among them.

"You can do anything, if you really want to," he said. "I wanted to do 'The 25th Hour' and with the help of God and Aunt Esther, I worked at it until I made it happen.

"I have this philosophy where there's no such thing as a stone wall, no such excuse as saying, 'I was going to do this, but I ran into a stone wall.' If you see yourself blocked, you think your problem through and look for another way; there's always another way."

When the fickleness of ill health blocked one way of life for Roy Siegel, he found another: With indomitable spirit, he looked grim fortune in the eye and smiled.

Rochelle Johnson

Greg and Rochelle Johnson on the White House lawn for the ceremony honoring Presidential Scholars (1985).

The features of character that defined Rochelle Johnson's long struggle were many, with courage, optimism, and faith among them. Yet stamina came nearest the heart of the matter, for it was with stamina that she sculpted an American success story from what could have been the common clay of failure.

Mrs. Johnson's idea of success was to make something of her four children, an ambition that some might have written off as hopeless because she was a low-income, black, divorced high school dropout living in a public housing project in Paducah, Kentucky.

But Rochelle would not accept suggestions that her kids already had three strikes against them; she went to bat for her children and made it a whole new ball game.

From the start she emphasized education, which she valued the more for having ended her own schooling at the tenth grade.

Mrs. Johnson saw to it that each of her children in turn, first Barbara, then Earl, then Gregory, then Bradford, was enrolled in a "readiness class" to prepare for the first grade.

"They usually started at the bottom of the class but ended at the top," she said.

It was a pattern of achievement that would be repeated time and again throughout the school years as Mrs. Johnson never tired of stressing the need to excel academically.

The children's academic struggles were played out against a backdrop of Rochelle's continuous financial struggles to provide for their needs.

Especially trying were the uncertain years immediately following her divorce, when Mrs. Johnson, confronting the world with four youngsters under the age of eight, felt compelled to make ends meet by accepting a limited amount of public assistance: food stamps and medical care for her children. This she did with considerable reluctance.

"When I was growing up, my parents said that man lives off the sweat of his own brow," she observed. "My mother and dad worked hard and didn't believe in taking anything they didn't work for. I didn't believe in it, either — thought it was demeaning. But pride wasn't going to feed or doctor the children, and I had to consider that. Also, I knew that taking this help was temporary; we weren't going to keep taking it."

To stay clear of welfare, Rochelle eventually decided she had to earn a predictable, dependable, adequate income by holding down two or more jobs at all times. For example, during the last several years that her kids were in school, she was working days as a teacher's aide and street-crossing guard, and nights as a cleaning lady.

"I get to school about a quarter to eight in the morning and work as a crossing guard so I can make some extra money," she said. "That goes to eight-thirty. Then I work as a teacher's aide until three o'clock, and a crossing guard again to three-thirty. From there, I go home, change, and report to my second job — for a cleaning service at a bank — by five o'clock. I work to nine unless somebody's out sick, in which case I work to ten. Then it's back home and to bed by midnight.

When she went to bat for her kids, it was a whole new ball game.

"I get up a little after six in the morning and leave an hour later," she continued. "I've been walking to work because my car's broken down again and I'll have to save up to fix it.

"But I don't much mind the walking. It's good exercise and gives me a chance to think, going along there when the world is just coming alive. That's a good time to walk. You can look at the trees, the birds, the sky, and see some of God's handiwork."

Rochelle said she hadn't always been a teacher's aide, crossing guard, and cleaning lady. Over the years she had also performed the duties of a maid, a domestic, and a nurse's aide, among other tasks.

Always, though, she had worked at least two jobs, always putting in days eighteen to twenty hours long. Nevertheless she still managed to provide stability in her children's homelife: sending them off to school in the morning, seeing them after school when she was between jobs, and making sure that they were tucked in when she herself fell into bed at the end of the day.

Mrs. Johnson's formula for pursuing her goal may have been simple: "You just work away, try not to get discouraged, and hope for the best." But it was far from easy.

"There were plenty of dark days, hard times," she confided. "There would be days that I was upset and tired out and wondering to myself, *Why are you going to all of this fuss and bother and endless work when you know you're going to die someday, anyway?*"

Then Rochelle would see her children progressing through school, piling success on success, and her question would answer itself.

"Barbara was a fine student. She graduated from high school and went right to the University of Kentucky," Mrs. Johnson said. "Earl did the same. In their way, they were trailblazers for the little ones. Barbara and Earl showed Greg and Brad that children from so-called underprivileged backgrounds could go to college."

The younger brothers took their siblings' formula and refined it.

Greg earned a straight-A grade average at Paducah's Tilghman High School on his way to becoming a Presidential Scholar (he and his mom were entertained by Ronald Reagan at the White House), a National Merit Scholarship finalist, and Tilghman's first-ever black valedictorian. He took a scholarship to Brown University and studied medicine at that Ivy League school.

The youngest of the four, Brad, all but mirrored Greg's performance, recording a straight-A average and becoming the second black valedictorian in Tilghman's history. He accepted an appointment to the United States Military Academy at West Point.

Thanks in no small measure to their own hard work and gifted intellect, outstanding success came to each of the Johnson children. Yet they and all who knew the family appreciated that their achievements must ultimately be credited to Rochelle.

Typical was the view of Anna McNabb, principal of the Paducah elementary school all of the Johnson children attended, who said that while the youngsters may have lacked material advantages, "they had a wealth of love and encouragement which pushed them to take advantage of every educational opportunity." They succeeded, she said, "because they had a mother who cared."

The view of Rochelle's children was summed up by Gregory, when he remarked that his mom had set them a great example. He said: "She inspired us with her stamina," meaning nearly two decades of long days, short nights, chronic fatigue, worry, and sacrifice.

Rochelle's response to well-deserved praise was invariably, and sincerely, humble. "I've never seen anything extraordinary in what I've done," she said. "For me, it was no more than what I should have done. I've been responsible for the children, their parent, and parents are supposed to do the very best that they can by their children. A lot of the time, we don't even *know* what the best is. We just try to do what we can, day by day.

"As for working two jobs, many people did that," she pointed out. "Besides, I was grateful to have two jobs when there were some people who had none. I thanked God for my two jobs.

"I have always thanked God for His blessings," she said in a soft, reflective voice. "My health is good, my children are doing well, and we all have food to eat and a roof over our heads. I know that none of these good things would have happened without God's help."

Something more that Rochelle Johnson knew was this: God helps those who help themselves.

Jerry Traylor

Many an endurance athlete never endured a 3,500-mile run across America. Jerry Traylor did.

Many a marathoner never completed almost three dozen of those 26-mile races. Jerry Traylor did.

Many a strong competitor never had the strength to race three times to the 14,110-foot top of Pikes Peak. Jerry Traylor did.

And he did it all on crutches.

"But it's not the crutches, not the difficulty that matters," said Jerry. "What counts is the *doing*."

Doing was essential to Jerry, thirty-one, of Parkersburg, West Virginia. Because during nearly half of his life, he'd been unable to do much of anything.

"For over fourteen years, I saw life pass me by," he said. "I was born with cerebral palsy and had over a dozen major corrective operations by my early teens.

"This meant I was in bed a lot of the time. When I was six, for example, I spent eleven months in a body cast that came clear up to here," he said, pointing to the middle of his chest. "I couldn't turn over or move by myself for all of that time — almost a year. After that until I was fourteen, I got around with steel leg braces that went from my waist to the soles of my feet."

Then Jerry Traylor was liberated; the braces came off and he was turned loose, with nothing to hold him back except crutches.

"What a thrill it was to get those crutches," he said. "I'm forever thankful for my crutches, because if I didn't have them, I'd simply fall down, but with them I can do things.

"You see, there are two kinds of crutches — positive and negative," he said. "Mine are positive crutches. They help me, support me, and free me to get out and live life. But crutches can be negative, too, if people *think* that they are and let the crutches limit them or handicap them."

Jerry's crutches did not handicap him. He went to college, earned a degree in business administration, and landed a position with the Treasury Department's Bureau of Public Debt. He also developed himself athletically and set about accomplishing increasingly difficult goals, such as running races on his crutches. Even so, Jerry felt compelled to do more.

"I quit my job with the government to become a motivational speaker," he said. "I wanted to tell people that all things are possible, that they could do anything — absolutely anything — if they would just give themselves a chance, and try.

"To be effective, though, I felt I'd have to establish myself not just as a motivational speaker, but a motivational *doer*, too."

Jerry decided he could make his point best by doing things people thought him incapable of doing.

He began running more marathons, and running them faster — setting an unofficial record when he finished one 26-mile jaunt on crutches in just five hours and nine minutes. He went up against and conquered the steep, rocky heights of Pikes Peak, then repeated the feat the next year, and the next.

Finally, he undertook the biggest physical challenge of his life: to run across America. Starting from San Francisco late one February, Jerry followed a serpentine route that he called "The Trail of New Beginnings" from coast to coast, arriving in New York City seven months and 3,500 miles later. He averaged about 15 miles a day and wore out two dozen pairs of shoes plus three pairs of crutches, along the way delivering about two hundred motivational speeches and raising large sums for charity.

While people who thought that he would never make it marveled at Jerry's extraordinary achievement, he said it represented no more than trying to reach his potential.

"I don't think anything I do is really that remarkable," he explained. "What's remarkable is life; that's totally remarkable. I think what I do is just to live life and make the best of every single thing the Lord has given me to use. So long as I keep trying, I don't worry about falling down. And believe me, there were plenty of times that I fell flat on my face."

But always, Jerry Traylor got back up and tried again.

Kirsten Halton

"It was at a high school basketball game up in Collinsville, I think," John Halton of Belleville, Illinois, was saying as he recon-

Kirsten Halton does a cheer.
(Belleville News Democrat/Brad Kellerman.)

structed the occasion in his mind.

"Our local kids from Belleville East High were the visiting team. I had gotten there late and ended up sitting in the Collinsville rooting section, where people wouldn't have known anything about the kids from Belleville.

"Anyway, I was watching the game and paying no attention to this couple in front of me until I noticed the husband nod his head toward the visitors' section and give his wife a little elbow in the ribs.

"He told her to look at the Belleville cheerleaders and said in kind of a whisper, 'Do you see that little girl over there? I've been watching her, and I think that little cheerleader's only got one leg.'

"'Naw,' answered the wife, 'that's impossible. How can you be a cheerleader with only one leg?'

"But when the woman turned and watched the cheerleaders for a few moments, she exclaimed, 'Oh, my goodness, yes! You're right, she *does* have just one leg! She's so graceful and natural, though, you'd never guess.'"

Knowing who the astonished couple were talking about before he even looked, John Halton joined them in directing an admiring gaze at this special cheerleader. But when he did, he could hardly see her through the sudden mist that he found himself brushing from his eyes, for the girl they spoke of, the petite cheerleader with one leg, was his daughter.

"I was always proud of Kirsten, but never more than at that moment, overhearing those people's wonder and admiration," John said. "My tears, I suppose, were a mix of sadness for her loss and pride for her toughness in facing more than her share of trouble."

But trouble hadn't always been Kirsten's lot. On the contrary, she had been just about every teenaged girl's self-dream: popular, talented, intelligent, and beautiful, with eyes and complexion and hair and features right out of the cosmetics commercials.

Then one day a few weeks after Kirsten turned sixteen, a doctor told her that a diagnosis of the pain in her right leg had confirmed everyone's worst suspicions. He said she had osteogenic sarcoma — bone cancer — and the only way to save her life was to sacrifice her leg.

The amputation, at mid-thigh, was done seven days later.

"For some reason, I wasn't frightened," Kirsten said. "Obviously, though, I was upset. When I was alone sometimes, I would cry and ask, 'Why me? Why me?'

"I didn't want anything to change. I wanted to go on being like everybody else. I was angry and frustrated that I might never cheerlead again."

"Don't worry, Daddy, I'm doing great...."

Kirsten forged her frustration (what her dad praised as her "orneriness") into a steel-edged determination to resume cheerleading, pick up her life, and move on with an optimism that sustained her and those around her through even the darkest days, days recalled by her father.

"In all sincerity, from the beginning I can't say there was ever a period when she was 'down,'" said John, a retired air force lieutenant colonel. "I don't know, she may have cried on her own when she was by herself, but she never let on to the family.

"Actually, I think we were the ones who were down," he went on. "Every time she had to go for follow-up bone scans and tests, I would sort of descend into the pit again and get depressed. I'd become worried and scared, waiting for a doctor to turn his eyes away from me and say, 'I'm afraid we've found another cancer.' That never happened, though I kept expecting it.

"But Kirsten's attitude was terrific, a source of real strength. She'd say, 'I don't know why you're worried, Daddy. I feel fine and I'm doing great.'"

In fact, she really was doing quite well, even if she didn't feel good much of the time because of chemotherapy treatments that sickened and weakened her for days on end and left her bald and wearing a wig for almost a year and a half. Nevertheless, Kirsten resumed her studies during convalescence and with extensive tutoring by her cheerleading coach, Margo Belt, kept academic pace with her high school class by passing all of her exams.

Yet the sternest test still lay before Kirsten. Having completed her physical rehabilitation, could she perform again as a cheerleader? Even if she could, would she really want to? Would a sensitive one-legged teenager have what it took to put herself on public display?

"She needed courage to get up and keep going after what she'd been through," said her father, "and she had that, thank God."

Despite some misgivings, Kirsten returned to the cheerleading squad that autumn and discovered that her doubts were mostly unfounded. With the exception of a few extremely difficult maneuvers which she could sit out, she found herself blending right in with the twelve-girl team's stunts and routines as though she had never been away. She was a full-fledged member again.

In a span of barely six months, Kirsten had made good on her vow, had returned, had gone from amputee to cheerleader once more.

"Imagine!" said coach Margo Belt. "She's out there in front of the public, without crutches or a prosthesis, completely on her own with one leg — doing back flips!"

And doing them perfectly.

For if Kirsten Halton weren't flawless, her extraordinary achievement would have been noticed by all of the fans, not just a few, like that couple her dad overheard at the game in Collinsville. That she was outstanding, yet did not stand out — even while standing on one leg — was a tribute to her fortitude and tenacity.

Margaret Patrick and Ruth Eisenberg

Margaret Patrick (foreground) and Ruth Eisenberg, sure to be a perfect pair, a match like ebony and ivory.

A true measure of human spirit is resiliency: not how hard people fall under the weight of crushing blows, but how high they rise in bouncing back.

Two who suffered catastrophic falls yet

managed to endure and rebound to inspiring heights were Margaret Patrick of Englewood, New Jersey, and Ruth Eisenberg from the nearby community of Cliffside Park. They were women who had never met but shared much in common, including the fact that both were incapacitated in the same year by the same kind of personal calamity, a stroke.

"Actually, my stroke came last, after I had two heart attacks," Mrs. Patrick, seventy-four, explained in words spoken clearly but slowly because of lingering stroke effects, which also included partial paralysis of her right hand.

"I had one heart attack, and when they were taking me to the hospital to treat that, I had a second one," she said. "Then while I was in the hospital, I had the stroke. I don't remember very much about it. The doctors said afterward that they never thought I would live. If I lived, they thought I wouldn't recover at all. But I had faith; I showed them. I thought to myself, *If it's to be, it's to be*, and I stopped worrying about it."

Meanwhile, a few miles away, Ruth Eisenberg was suffering a similar experience. Ruth, eighty-five, recalled that her stroke had crippled virtually one-half of her body. "It hit my whole left side — face, tongue, arm, hand, everything," she said.

"To this day, five years later, the side of my face feels like I just came from the dentist — numb. My speech used to be very slurred. But I worked hard on it, did a lot of rehabilitation, and got better. One of the therapists who took an interest in me was a woman specializing in phonetic articulatory pathology. I guess if I can say *phonetic articulatory pathology*, she succeeded at her job," Ruth joked.

However, there was no joking about the rest of Ruth's recovery, which didn't fare nearly as well as her speech. "My left hand is functionally useless," she said. "I have some sensation, but no dexterity." Moreover, she lost much of her mobility.

"It was devastating, absolutely debilitating," Mrs. Eisenberg said. "I was so depressed and full of sympathy for myself that I didn't want anyone to see me walk with a walker or a cane or use the wheelchair. I stayed in the house for weeks on end and thought about nothing but myself.

A musical match made in heaven.

"The worst of it, though, was that I couldn't play the piano anymore," she continued. "I tried, but found it very depressing to play and hear only half of the music. It was disheartening not to be able to do a little Bach, or even a little rock, after having played for so many years."

Until she had her stroke, Ruth had been playing for almost sixty years, ever since her late husband, Jacob, had taught her how as a young woman.

"My husband was a writer. He wrote textbooks to teach adults how to learn to play the piano, and I became his laboratory," she said. "He had his own methods, and he used these with me to illustrate what the adult mind could accomplish with proper instruction. In the beginning I didn't want to study. Ultimately, however, to please him, I learned to play and I became a willing student in the end. Eventually, I got to love it."

Margaret Patrick also loved music, and at the time of her stroke, she also had been playing for some sixty years, although she came to it not with reluctance but enthusiasm. She began piano lessons at the age of eight and went on to teach piano herself and play professionally as an accompanist for vocalists and local orchestras. Just as Ruth did, Margaret also missed the piano terribly.

Deprived of their music and some of their faculties, Mrs. Patrick and Mrs. Eisenberg turned, separately, to the Southeast Senior Center for Independent Living in Englewood. They were drawn to the center to rebuild their battered bodies, but what happened there started them rebuilding their battered spirits.

"I went to a therapy class at the center one day, and they had a piano there," Ruth said. "I hadn't been playing at all. I was listless and gloomy. So I wandered over to the piano and began to play, with just one finger," she said. "I was plinking away, feeling sorry for myself, when a group director from the center — a woman named Millie McHugh — came over and introduced this other lady to me."

The other lady was Margaret Patrick.

As Ruth recalled the incident, "Millie said to me, 'The two of you have some things in common: Margaret plays the piano, too, and she also had a stroke, but on the opposite side to yours. Why don't the two of you get together?'

"I said, 'Why not?'"

The two women arranged themselves at the keyboard — Margaret with her good left hand over the bass keys, Ruth with her good right hand over the treble keys — and slowly began to play.

It took only a few moments to discover that they had similar repertoires anchored strongly in the classics and that each woman's strengths complemented the other's weaknesses. In a short while, the spirited strains of Chopin's "Minute Waltz" filtered through the center. These were followed by works from Brahms, Bach, Beethoven, and other giants of the keyboard.

As they played, the women talked, and learned of the remarkable similarities in their lives. Not only were they both recovering stroke victims who had played the piano for most of their lives; both also were widows and great-grandmothers who even shared the same astrological sign: Gemini, the twins.

For all of their likenesses, however, there were also some striking differences between Margaret and Ruth.

Margaret tended to be shy, staid, and reserved, while Ruth was fast-talking, gregarious, and outgoing. Margaret moved about on her own, but Ruth had to use a walker or wheelchair. Margaret was slender and conservative of dress, while Ruth tended toward plumpness and sported bright colors. At the keyboard, of course, Margaret was the left hand, Ruth the right hand.

And it was in those hands that the starkest difference of all could be seen: Margaret played with five black fingers, while Ruth played with five white fingers.

"We called ourselves Ebony and Ivory, like the black and white keys of the piano. We got right into the music, and we've been playing ever since," said Ruth.

"Margaret and I started by giving recitals at the senior center, to help people there by showing them what we could do — not just coping with strokes but also with stubborn arthritis, which I have in my right hand. That's when things began to change in my life," Ruth continued. "When I stopped thinking about me and started thinking about other people, that's when I got around to feeling better myself. I tell that to people whenever the two of us perform."

Over the years, Ruth and Margaret performed often, appearing before audiences small and large, including those of some national television programs. They varied their music, drawing mostly from the classics, with occasional ventures into the popular arena, but their message was always the same: "To demonstrate what motivation can do," Ruth explained. "To show what you can achieve with the right attitude."

"Encouragement," Margaret added. "When we play for the disabled, it encourages them a lot. They see us and think maybe if they try, then they can do things, too. After we performed recently, a man who had had a stroke came up to the piano and said we inspired him. He played a little bit with his good hand, and we told him to keep playing and not let it waste away. He said he would."

Since Margaret was stronger of hand while Ruth was stronger of voice, Ruth assumed the task of engaging the audience verbally.

"Before the program, I generally take the audience on a little adventure in music," she noted. "I go into the life of the composers, talk about how Beethoven went deaf but still continued to compose, and then discuss something about the pieces we'll be playing.

"During the performance, if something goes wrong or if I get into trouble with the music, to stall for time I might tell a story that verges on being wicked," Ruth chuckled, with eyes twinkling. "Margaret is very dignified, and she sometimes becomes apprehensive about what I'm about to say. But of course I keep everything in good taste. Once in a while, though, when things are going well and I get a bit overexuberant or enthusiastic, I might blurt out something like 'Hot damn!' Then Margaret clucks her tongue and says, 'Oh, dear!' and we laugh. I guess we sort of complement each other," Ruth Eisenberg said, with straight-faced understatement.

For it seemed clear to all who witnessed the activities of these remarkable women that so graceful, so natural, so symmetrical — so perfect— was their harmonious union that it might have been divinely ordained, a musical match made in heaven. And who was to say otherwise? Not Margaret Patrick.

"Sometimes, something good comes out of something bad," she said. Then, feeling for words, Margaret attempted to recite a proverb that a doctor had encouraged her with during her stroke rehabilitation.

"God never closes ..." she started, then hesitated.

"God never closes a door but He opens a window?" someone prompted.

"That's it," she said. "God put us together. When I needed a good right hand, He sent me Ruth."

VOLUNTEERISM

Americans have never much liked being told or directed or ordered to do anything. But they have always loved to volunteer.

Indeed, the nation itself was born of the sacrifice and blood of volunteers: those who battled for freedom in the Revolutionary War. And the national fondness for volunteering, as an expression of personal involvement in the life of the community and the country, has persisted ever since, throughout all our days.

Just as the renowned French political commentator Alexis de Tocqueville marveled at what he called "the spirit of volunteerism in America" during a visit here early in the last century, so observers still marvel at the extent to which ordinary citizens by the tens of millions contribute their time, talent, toil, and sweat working for relief of the individual or improvement of the common good. By some estimates, almost half of all Americans older than their mid-teens regularly devote at least a few hours to working without pay for the benefit of others, whether in schools, hospitals, churches, civic organizations, emergency services, or a multitude of other endeavors. Their donated time mounts into the billions of hours every year.

The word *volunteer* stems from an ancient root meaning "free will." The accounts that follow tell about some of the ways contemporary Americans go about volunteering — working not at the dictates of others, but of their own free will. By their examples, they inspire us all.

John Penne

"It was September 26, 1985," said John Penne. "I was driving and stopped for a red light. That's all I remember. When I came to, it was October.

"I really never knew what hit me, but they said afterward that a truck pulling a seven-ton earth mover on a flatbed trailer came alongside me and somehow the earth mover fell off the trailer, smack onto my station wagon.

"The lady who was riding with me at the time wasn't hurt, but I was in pretty bad shape: fractured skull, crushed sinuses, broken jaw, other injuries, too. They told me it took the rescue workers an hour and a half to get me out of the wreck.

"I woke up in the hospital eight or nine days later and spent three more weeks there, plus two weeks in rehabilitation. Then I was six months recuperating."

The combination of a close brush with death, a slow recovery, and a fast-approaching seventy-first birthday might have convinced some men to abandon their cars once and for all. But not John. As soon as he was able, he was back behind the wheel, driving as always.

For John, who lived in suburban Milwaukee, Wisconsin, was a man with a driving mission, a mission he had dedicated the rest of his life to and was itching to resume ever since it had been interrupted that September day when the world fell in on him.

In fact, it was in the performance of his mission that John had been nearly killed in the first place, since he was stopped in traffic at that fateful moment when the earth mover toppled onto his car only because he was driving a cancer patient — the woman who escaped injury in the accident — to a hospital for chemotherapy treatment.

That was John Penne's everyday mission of mercy.

It was something he had been working at for many years, six or seven hours a day, five days a week, as a full-time volunteer driver for the American Cancer Society.

He had donated thousands of hours and tens of thousands of hard-driving miles so people undergoing the rigors of extended cancer treatment might avoid the added rigors of extended waiting for transportation to or from the hospital.

John knew firsthand that the lives of cancer patients were difficult enough without these additional burdens: In the span of a few months during 1973, both he and his wife, Wanda, were stricken with colon cancer.

The symmetry of the cruel coincidence ended there, however, because while surgery eradicated John's cancer, Wanda was not so fortunate. She needed both surgery and follow-up treatment.

So John sold the tavern he had owned for

more than twenty-five years and devoted himself to looking after his wife: keeping house, cooking meals, tending to Wanda's every need, and frequently driving her to and from chemotherapy or radiation sessions at the hospital.

It was during these visits that John and Wanda became aware of the many patients — nauseated, weakened, miserable from the effects of potent anti-cancer regimens — who lingered for hours in waiting rooms until friends or relatives could come to drive them home.

Although Wanda did not have to endure the waiting, she did endure the treatments. And with John at her side, she fought bravely against cancer through several hospitalizations. But the long battle was ultimately a losing one. About four years after the struggle started, she was back in the hospital once again and fading.

"The doctor took me aside and told me, 'There's nothing more that we can do for Wanda here in the hospital. I think you should take her home, where she can be more comfortable and things will be easier on both of you,'" John related.

"When I got her home, she knew how things were working out. She didn't see any reason to think she could keep going on much longer. We were sitting at home there talking one day, and she asked me, 'John, what are you going to do when I'm gone?'

"'Well,' I said, 'the Cancer Society's been looking for volunteer drivers. After what's happened to you and me, I think maybe I'm going to go and do that.'

"She said, 'It's nice that you'll be taking care of people that need help.'

"She felt real good knowing what I'd be doing."

Six weeks later, Wanda's life ended.

And John's mission began.

Maria Snidle

Maria Snidle is honored in recognition of her 15,000 hours of voluntary service to DePaul Hospital in Norfolk, Virginia.

Somebody suggested it was a job that couldn't be filled for love or money: hospital work from five in the morning until two in the afternoon, six days a week, weekends and holidays included. But the suggestion was wrong, because while it was probable that no one would have done the work for money, someone did it for love.

Maria Snidle was her name.

"I do my work because I love God and I love people, love to *be* with people," said Maria, a volunteer of long standing at DePaul

Hospital in Norfolk, Virginia, where she made her home. "I wouldn't like to have money for this. What I can do for God and people, I can do for nothing."

Without material reward of any sort, Maria — a grandmother whose youthful appearance belied her sixty-five years — toiled for God and for people week in and week out for over a dozen years, revealing a level of dedication that was matched by the level of her sacrifice.

"I'm up at four o'clock every morning," she said, meaning Tuesday through Sunday, since she sometimes slept in until five or six on Monday, her day off. "After I say my prayers and get dressed, I leave and reach the hospital at about five. I start by seeing if anyone wants coffee or newspapers or breakfast, which I take to them.

"At six o'clock I go to the hospital chapel for Mass," she went on. "When that is over I help the sisters clean the chapel and then help the priest bring communion to the patients that want it. Then I spend the rest of the day doing whatever the patients and staff need.

"I bring meals and magazines and books, deliver hospital records, help lady patients fix their hair, get coffee for visitors, read or write letters for some patients, just talk or listen to other ones. Whatever I can do, I'm happy. Big thing, small thing, no matter.

"The people in the hospital, they need lots of love," said Maria, a naturalized American whose warmly accented English suggested her Italian heritage. "They are ill, they are lonely. They need comfort and understanding, someone to talk to — especially the people with cancer."

Mrs. Snidle had a special feeling and place in her heart for cancer victims; having been one herself, she was in a position to serve as a compassionate counselor and confidante.

"I listen to people with cancer and try to tell them not to be afraid," she said. "Fear is the worst thing about cancer. But when patients hear about my cancer and my experience, they ask me to come and talk to them. I tell them that if they have faith, then cancer is not the end of the world. I say to them that they can still live and do a lot of things."

Stopping for a lengthy pause, Maria continued: "It is very hard for me to go into this subject, because I had the breast cancer and every time I talk about it to someone, I think again about the suffering I went through — the surgery [a radical double mastectomy], the chemotherapy, and everything else.

"It is not easy, but I talk about it because it helps someone worse off than me.

"My reward is that I am able to pull their spirits up, and they feel better after we talk," she remarked. "Sometimes they call me at home and ask me to explain this and that about cancer. After they have breast cancer surgery, I tell the women how to do their exercises for recovery.

"I tell everybody that I had cancer but I am still alive and never felt so good in my life as now. Since my breast cancer, I became more strong," Maria said.

"What I'm doing is sharing my blessings."

"It was a big operation and I thought I was dead, but God saved me. He could have taken my life, because I see many people my age with cancer who are without hope. They just go. But God gave me life — four years already. I feel so good and so fortunate, I am blessed. What I am doing here at DePaul is sharing my blessings."

In addition to her recovery from cancer, Maria counted among her blessings three grown children, five grandchildren, and four decades of marriage to Ernest Snidle, the navy radioman she met in her native Naples and later wed. He now was retired from the service and employed as an educator.

Mrs. Snidle said Ernest strongly encouraged her volunteer effort and never felt neglected because she saw to it that even if she was not on hand, anything he might need was in easy reach.

"I always have everything in order, everything in the right place, all very neat," she said. "If I am not here, his dinner is still ready. All he has to do is put it in the microwave and warm it."

Maria explained that although she completed her hospital duties at two o'clock, there were times she was away during her free hours performing other volunteer tasks — among them chauffeuring the elderly to and from errands and serving as an interpreter for Italian or Spanish merchant seamen who spoke no English.

Even her supposed "day off" from DePaul frequently was spent in service to others.

"When the schools are open, I go once a month on Monday to volunteer at Holy Trinity School [a parochial school in Norfolk]," she said. "I watch over the little children who come to the infirmary. Any Monday I am there, the children all want to be sick so they can go to the infirmary and I can care for them," Maria related, her voice filled with pleasure.

"They say, 'Oh, I don't feel good. My stomach is sick. My head aches. My knee is sore.' So I take their temperatures, feel their foreheads, fix their knees, give them juice and cookies. But what they really want is to be babied," she smiled.

"I can never find enough things to do to help people," Mrs. Snidle observed. "There is always more to do.

"Sometimes when I wake up in the morning, the thought is in my head that maybe I'm feeling sick. I say to myself, *I'd better stay home.* Five o'clock in the morning until two o'clock in the afternoon is a lot of work for a lady sixty-five years old. I'm tired. I don't sleep much all night because I worry about the patients. But then I get out of bed and say, 'No. I must go. I'm wanted. I'm needed, even by the people that aren't sick,'" she said.

"A few days ago, a nurse comes to me in the hospital. She is crying. She says she needs help. We go to the lounge, and we talk. After some time, finally she tells me what the matter is. 'Something is wrong with my breast, a lump,' she says. She is scared to death of cancer. She is afraid to find out.

"I tell her to go for a checkup and it turns out okay. The lump, it is nothing," Maria Snidle said. "She is so happy, and I am happy for her.

"I am happy for me, too. Because she is a nurse and I am nothing, just a volunteer. But still she comes to me for help. I feel good about this because people have faith in me, trust me, and know that I am happy and grateful to be able to help them.

"The people see what I do. They understand me. They read my heart."

What they read there was a message in one word: love.

Aubrey McDonald

Worthwhile volunteering makes no demands for sparkling brilliance or inspiration, refined skill or talent, abundant time or money.

"What you need is to care about people and want to help them," said Aubrey "Mac" McDonald. "If you're friendly, you can do a whole lot."

With a limited investment of time and money but a large investment of care and friendship, Mac did much over the years to diminish a silent terror that haunted many isolated residents in Duncanville, Texas, the Dallas suburb where he lived with his wife of a half-century, Peggy.

The seldom-mentioned but always-present terror that stalked numerous elderly and homebound individuals was the prospect of a sickness or injury that could leave them to suffer and die alone.

Without families, lacking resources to hire companions, yet determined to remain independent, they lived with the constant fear of a mishap — a crippling fall, a sudden illness — that might incapacitate them.

What they needed was someone to help, someone to care: a friend. In Mac McDonald, they found a friend. More correctly, he found them.

"I'd done some reading about this problem with these older people," said Mac, who put in five days a week at his tool and hardware business, even though he was in his mid-seventies. "I worked up an idea for dealing with the situation, wrote it out, and presented it to the Duncanville Police Department. They approved it."

The plan okayed by the police was dubbed CALM, which stood for "Call and Leave Message." Mac founded CALM on the sensible belief that a minute of caring was worth a month of curing.

"Every morning from seven-thirty to eight-thirty," he said, "I sit by my phone waiting to spend a minute or two with each of the people who've signed up for the CALM program with the police department. There are fifteen or so elderly. The police have done all of the legwork, finding out who wants to take part, what their problems are, what medical background they have, and so forth.

"Anyhow, during this hour each morning, all of these people call and check in with me. If they don't phone me," he continued, "I contact them. Usually I find out that they've just forgotten to call, and they apologize. But if I get no answer, then I make an emergency call according to whatever setup has been okayed in advance.

"To give you an idea," Mac said, "there recently was this ninety-one-year-old lady who'd been in the program for several years. She was very good about calling, but this one morning she didn't. So I dialed her number and let it ring fifteen or twenty times. No answer.

"I checked and saw that the plan was to alert a neighbor. I called him. He went to her house, looked through a window, and saw her lying there, not moving."

The neighbor telephoned police and medics, who entered her home. Inside, they found that the woman had suffered a stroke and was in a coma. She recovered in the hospital.

"That's exactly the kind of thing I'm trying to do with CALM," Mac observed. "I want to make sure that nobody's left lying on the floor somewhere for a day or a week, suffering and helpless."

However, the efforts of Mac and Peggy provided more than reassurance against medical catastrophes. They provided vital companionship as well.

"A lot of these people hardly ever get out of their homes," he explained. "On many days, the only person they have a chance to talk to is me or my wife. We always chat with them as long as we can and make sure everything's okay.

"The first thing we ask is, 'Are you all right?' Then, 'Do you need anything?' Then we ask about any problems they may have. Often, they're struggling with little difficulties that they don't know how to handle. I don't always know how, either, but I do know how to reach someone who can get the answer for them.

"None of this is a big deal," Aubrey McDonald said, "but it's important to them, so that makes it important to me. I like helping them."

And he did a lot of it. Over the years, no fewer than forty-two thousand project CALM phone calls were handled by this man whose acquaintances knew him as "Mac," but whose clients knew him as "friend."

Lucille Starr

Lucille Starr at her desk.

Three or four days a week during most weeks of the year, Lucille Starr of Daytona Beach, Florida, did volunteer work for a local charity. She would make her way to the organization's office and spend several hours there answering phones, filing papers, stuffing envelopes, running errands, doing whatever she could to promote the cause.

Then she would return home — not to relax, but to resume a long-standing volunteer commitment that was so strenuous that working for charity became her idea of taking a breather.

"My letter writing is hard work, plain and simple," observed Mrs. Starr. "It saps me, it drains me physically and emotionally," she said of her effort to reach, to comfort, to touch society's "untouchables," men and women in prisons and penitentiaries across America.

"These people are cut off, lonely, hurt," she said. "Many have been abandoned by their families — just dropped, cast aside. They have nobody."

Nobody except Lucille, a youthful-looking woman in her mid-sixties who spent years breaking through the isolation of prison inmates by carrying on a prodigious correspondence with them.

"I write individual letters to about 150 prisoners, some once a month but most twice a month," she said. "Every month, I do about 225 letters. But I don't think about it that way — as 225 letters. I do them one at a time, so it doesn't seem like so much work.

"I want to see them go to heaven rather than hell."

"A few are typed," Mrs. Starr went on, "but the majority are written by hand and are usually about four pages long. It takes me maybe five or six hours a day to keep up with this, because these are not easy letters to write. Pretty often I cry over them, because I feel how much these people are hurting.

"A lot of them ask in their letters if they can call me Mom. It's generally the younger ones. That gets to me sometimes," said Lucille, the mother of two grown children and wife of a retired federal employee. "I suppose when your family has dropped you, it helps to be able to write somebody and say, 'Dear Mom.' I always tell them I enjoy being called Mom." Lucille said she enjoyed it even though the person doing the calling might be a robber, rapist, or murderer.

"Some prisoners tell me that they have done the most horrible things, but I try not to judge them. Society has already done that. I only want to let them know that somebody cares. I want to see them go to heaven rather than hell," Mrs. Starr observed. "That's the whole purpose of all this writing.

"It started about eight years ago when I was listening to a preacher over the radio. On this program every day, he would answer letters that prisoners had written in.

"I thought to myself, *Could I do that?* I prayed about it and then took down off the air some names and addresses of inmates who wanted letters. At first I was scared," she said. "I didn't know how to write, what to say.

"My first letter was to this young guy in Asheville, North Carolina. I got a nice reply. After that, I just kept at it, and every time I wrote a letter to someone new, it got a little easier."

Eventually, her correspondence grew to where she was writing more than 2,500 letters a year to hardened desperadoes and minor criminals, life termers and short timers. What she got from them was loneliness, frustration, and despair; what they got from her was companionship, encouragement, and hope.

However, she prudently drew the line at letters, pointing out that she never answered their requests for money or anything else material. "You have to be careful that you're not used. These guys can take you for all you're worth if you don't watch out," she said in a manner which made it clear that

Lucille's softness was in her heart, not her head.

Even so, she said her work met with less than universal approval. "My husband isn't so enthusiastic about what I do, but he tolerates it because he knows it's the Lord's work," she confided. "Also, there were some people I once knew who stopped talking to me because I corresponded with criminals. That used to bother me a lot, but it doesn't anymore. I'm a happy person for it all.

"I love what I'm doing, even if the people I've been writing to were criminals. They all did hateful things," she noted, "but I told them that God still loved them."

With her toil and tears, Lucille Starr also told them that God was not alone.

Dan Jacobson

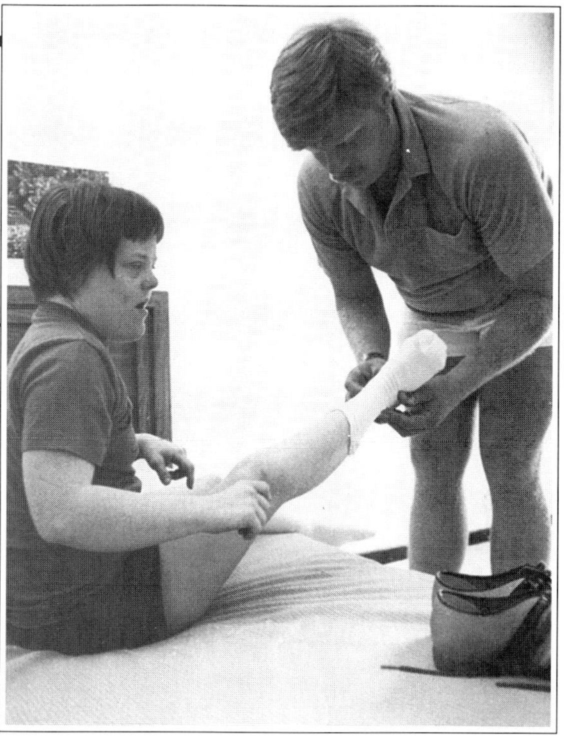

Dan Jacobson helps a youngster at the Nevada Rehabilitation Center to learn basic skills, like combing hair, brushing teeth, and putting on socks and shoes. (Jim Laurie/Las Vegas Review Journal.)

Dan Jacobson crouched beside a house trailer that served as the sales office for a used-car lot in Las Vegas, Nevada.

Clenched in his hand was a Smith & Wesson nine-millimeter semiautomatic pistol, standard issue of the Las Vegas Metropolitan Police, whose uniform Dan wore.

Facing him twenty feet away was his partner, Detective Lannis Mills, dressed in plain clothes. Their eyes were fixed on the office door that stood midway between them.

Suddenly, a man burst through that door, wheeled toward Mills, and opened fire with a handgun.

"I saw a muzzle flash, heard a pop, saw my partner go down," Dan Jacobson recalled. "It looked like Mills was hit, though he was moving, crawling. It raced through my mind that this suspect had just shot down a police officer, my partner, and now he was fixing to kill him.

"I had to prevent that. I opened up on the guy and didn't stop till he went down. I fired eleven rounds, hit him seven times.

"My partner, who hadn't been wounded after all but was diving for cover, fired ten shots and hit the suspect with one. The suspect — wanted for attempted murder, armed robbery, and auto theft — got off three shots before he was killed. So there were twenty-four shots in all. The whole thing took less than three seconds. Three seconds to end a life. He forced me to kill him, and it disgusted me."

That terrifying picture of compressed violence in Dan Jacobson's frontline fight against murderers and muggers, hoodlums and hookers, pushers and pimps stood out in stunning contrast to another fight he waged.

This was the gentle, slow, good fight that he carried on over many years as a volunteer working with profoundly retarded children at the Desert Development Center in Las Vegas.

"I handle the most severely mentally handicapped kids," Dan said. "These are the children who usually can't speak, can't take care of themselves, and often have to wear diapers, even though they may be fifteen or sixteen years old. One day a week I work with them on a lot of different things, but mostly on coping activities — skills they need to function in life at a minimal level. So we practice things like dressing ourselves, washing up, brushing our teeth, combing our hair, eating our meals," he explained.

"It might take some of these children an hour for something an average kid could do in a minute. But when they do it, it's a real accomplishment. It's a move toward independence. Some of them won't ever be able to achieve that, but some will — and do. When they show they can manage, they're moved into more advanced dormitories where they do things for themselves, like cooking their own meals."

How did a tough cop come to the business of tender care at a state institution?

"I was in the area on patrol one day," said Dan, who was thirty-one and single. "I walked in and signed up as a volunteer. To tell you the truth, I needed this. I needed some balance in my life. As you know, there's quite a bit of violence in police work. A lot of guys get themselves trapped into living and breathing this stuff twenty-four hours a day, until it starts to affect how they see things.

"This regular, everyday diet of crime and violence begins to distort their view of life and wear them down. I felt that way. I felt I needed something that could temporarily take me away from this."

So every Tuesday Dan put his gun and badge aside and exchanged his police uniform for tennis shorts, a polo shirt, and sneakers. Then he headed for the development center and a refresher course on life.

"Working with these kids reassures me that there are good things in the world worth fighting for," he observed. "I learn something new every time I visit the center — something about the good side of human nature, because these kids have all kinds of handicaps, but yet they don't give up. For them, it's a major achievement just to learn to tie their shoes. They might not ever get it right, but they keep at it. They want to live and grow like other kids.

"And they're always so gentle and affectionate," Dan went on. "Some people think the retarded lack all sensibilities, but that's not so. Their higher functions may be damaged, but they have strong affections and good memories.

Tough cop, tender care.

"There was a case where I hadn't visited one particular dormitory for some months. A boy I had worked with in the past had since moved in there. He was about eighteen years old, had Down's syndrome, couldn't speak, was hard of hearing, and couldn't see very well. But when I returned there and walked through the dorm close enough for him to see who I was, the first thing he did was grin, jump up, put his arm around me, and start following me all over as in the past. He wanted me to give him piggyback rides like when he was little. He didn't let me out of his sight for the twenty minutes I was there.

"These kids are slower than most, but they need and give love like any others," he said. "They provide me with a good, healthy balance to my life. They put my police work in perspective. They help me keep my sense of humanity. I don't want to lose that. Once you lose your humanity as a policeman, you deteriorate."

But Dan Jacobson didn't deteriorate, as a policeman or as a man. On the contrary, he flourished under the gentle influence of some special kids. Their natural innocence kept Dan's heart open to what was good in the world; his own savvy inner sense kept his eyes open to what was not.

Harry Saina

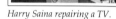

Harry Saina repairing a TV.

One of the attractions — and strengths — of volunteerism in America is the individuality it permits.

No matter where people's interests or talents point, there usually is a place for them in the framework of volunteering. As a consequence, individuals in cities and towns, villages and rural areas across the nation routinely apply themselves to tasks that fall outside the "mainstream" of volunteering but nevertheless meet important needs. Though the scope of their efforts is narrow and the numbers they reach are small, these volunteers give added dimension to the lives they touch.

"Happiness," said Harry Saina. "Happiness is what I try to give. Companionship, too," he added, as he took a break one evening to chat about the personal volunteer project he'd been working on for most of a decade in his community of Chester, Pennsylvania.

"My people for the most part are isolated, lonely, probably a little depressed," he said, making reference to the shut-ins, senior citizens, and disabled individuals who benefited from Harry's offer of free equipment repairs for folks who lacked the means, physical or financial, to get their broken radios, televisions, phonographs, and similar devices fixed in the usual way.

"For many of them, a TV or radio is all they have to keep them company. It's their only source of happiness, their only link to the world," he added. "If that conks out, then they're left all alone."

And alone was how they frequently remained until they met Harry — a thirty-nine-year-old electronics technician who lived in Chester with his wife, daughter, mother, and mother-in-law.

By day, he plied his trade as a professional; by night and on weekends, as a volunteer.

"I started out at this in a small way," he explained, "mostly just assisting an older person now and then with a broken set."

Soon, however, he became aware of a broader need for this kind of help for people whose poor health, handicaps, or meager resources prevented them from seeking repairs for these common but crucial appliances.

"At first, I took referrals from some social agencies. Then I expanded by distributing printed fliers offering my services to senior centers and places like that," Harry said. "I now do a couple of hundred jobs a year.

"Often, the people bring the broken equipment in and I fix it at my place. Otherwise, I make a house call and work on it there, or if it's too much to do there, put it in my car and bring it home. When it's done, I deliver it."

Harry's fee for this service, to which he devoted about thirty hours a week, was usually nothing. Sometimes, though, if he had to buy an exotic part that couldn't be appropriated from cast-off equipment that he fixed up and donated to social service agencies, he would assess his "customer" the wholesale price of the part. But for Harry's labor, expertise, sophisticated equipment, time, and trouble, there was never a charge.

"If you're helping from your heart, you don't care about your pocket," Harry Saina remarked. "You go and you see someone cooped up in a house or confined to a bed. They can't get out, can't do anything, can't go anywhere. They're by themselves and don't have any family," he said.

"If I fixed a radio or TV that wasn't working, or brought them a refurbished set they never had before, that would give them some company, some enjoyment. It would take them beyond those four blank walls."

And, it would add dimension to their lives.

Ray Mienheartt

The philosophy behind Dr. Ray Mienheartt's volunteering was practical and simple: "You can only do what you can do," he said.

"People in poor countries *need* everything, but I can't *do* everything. I can't build bridges or put up houses or drain swamps. Therefore, I do what I *can* do and give what I *can* give.

"The one really useful thing that I have to share is my skill as a vision specialist, my ability to help people see. So that's what I give," said Ray (whose last name was pronounced *mine*-heart and not, as it might have appeared, *mean*-heart, which was fitting, since mean heartedness was not in his nature).

Dr. Mienheartt, sixty-two, a Brazil, Indiana, optometrist, had been giving freely of his vision testing and correcting skills to Third World people for more than a decade, ever since joining Volunteer Optometric Services to Humanity (VOSH). VOSH is a nationwide organization of about three thousand members, mostly optometrists but also some ophthalmologists (medical doctors specializing in eye care) and lay people.

"The whole idea behind VOSH is to provide vision care for the poorest of the poor in all the emerging nations around the world," he pointed out. "These are people who have absolutely no vision services available to them. And if they did have, they wouldn't be able to afford them, anyway.

"My own experience has come from taking part in a dozen individual VOSH missions over the years, to countries in Central and South America. Our work on these ventures has been done wherever a lot of poor people could be brought together — in remote jungle villages, leper colonies, even prisons.

"When VOSH members go on a mission, to Guatemala or Honduras for instance," he said, "we take literally tons of testing equipment and eyeglasses with us. There are eight or ten of us optometrists and maybe an ophthalmologist, plus some support staff, and we spend one solid week there, with each doctor examining as many as a hundred patients a day. This means that among us, we're seeing something like a thousand people a day for an entire week.

"They come from everywhere, often walking forty miles or more through the jungles to reach us. I remember one doctor telling of a patient who said he had trekked over three hundred miles!"

Ray explained that since most of the patients he and his colleagues saw were illiterate peasants, traditional reading-based eye tests were of little value in assessing their vision.

"So we use more practical methods," he said. "We pour some grains of rice into a bowl along with a few bits of dirt and then ask the patients to separate the grain from the grit." Those who saw well enough to perform that function passed, while those who couldn't were tested further and fitted with glasses.

Of course, the examinations and the glasses were free, Dr. Mienheartt noted. He said VOSH members provided all professional services without charge and paid for mission expenses, including travel and related costs, out of their own pockets.

Not a missionary — but a visionary.

The glasses could be given away, he said, because they were usable castoffs donated by the American public to ongoing collection campaigns conducted by Lions clubs, Rotary clubs, and participating eye-care specialists.

As for VOSH itself, Dr. Mienheartt said the organization accepted no outside funding and was maintained entirely through the support of its members, most of whom were committed for the long term. Typically, he said, members returned to participate in overseas VOSH missions annually, as he himself had done twelve times in twelve years.

"These missions are like those potato chips they advertise," he quipped. "You can't take just one. You go once, and you're hooked. It gets in your blood. It calls you back again and again, because you see poverty the like of which you never imagined in your life.

"Every veteran of a VOSH mission has at least one story that sticks in his craw and stays with him forever. Myself, I'll never forget the time that we visited a hospital in Honduras. It was a really poor hospital and had no supplies, not even aspirin! We went into the children's section and saw all these little kids lying there on plastic covers with no sheets.

"I noticed one terribly emaciated little boy whose black hair was turning reddish, which meant he was dying of malnutrition. A doctor said the kid was past saving, so we gave him the only thing we had — a lollipop. He tasted it and smiled, probably his last smile, because he was dead the next day. We returned to that area several times, but I could never forget that little boy, and I couldn't bring myself to visit that particular hospital again."

VOSH stories were not usually so sad, however. In fact, most were happy, involving thousands of people with routine vision problems easily fixed, and occasionally something more dramatic.

"Once in a while, we'd run into a kid who everybody in the village thought was blind," said Ray. "But on examination it turned out that he wasn't blind at all. He just had really poor vision that we could correct with very, very powerful glasses — you know, 'Coke bottle' lenses.

"Watching people see for the first time in their lives is a wonderful, intensely moving experience."

Ray said the pure joy of experiences like that kept the VOSH volunteers coming back year after year, just as the pure altruism of their work kept them out of trouble, even in troubled lands.

"We hardly ever run into problems, and that's because we have no political or religious affiliation whatsoever," he said. "Remember: We're not missionaries, we're visionaries."

And so they were. Ray Mienheartt and the quiet volunteers of VOSH didn't want to change the world; they just wanted to help people see it.

AMERICAN SCENES & CELEBRATIONS

**Hail, Columbia! happy land!
Hail, ye heroes!
heaven-born band!
Who fought and bled in
Freedom's cause.**

*JOSEPH HOPKINSON
Hail, Columbia*

nald's

80

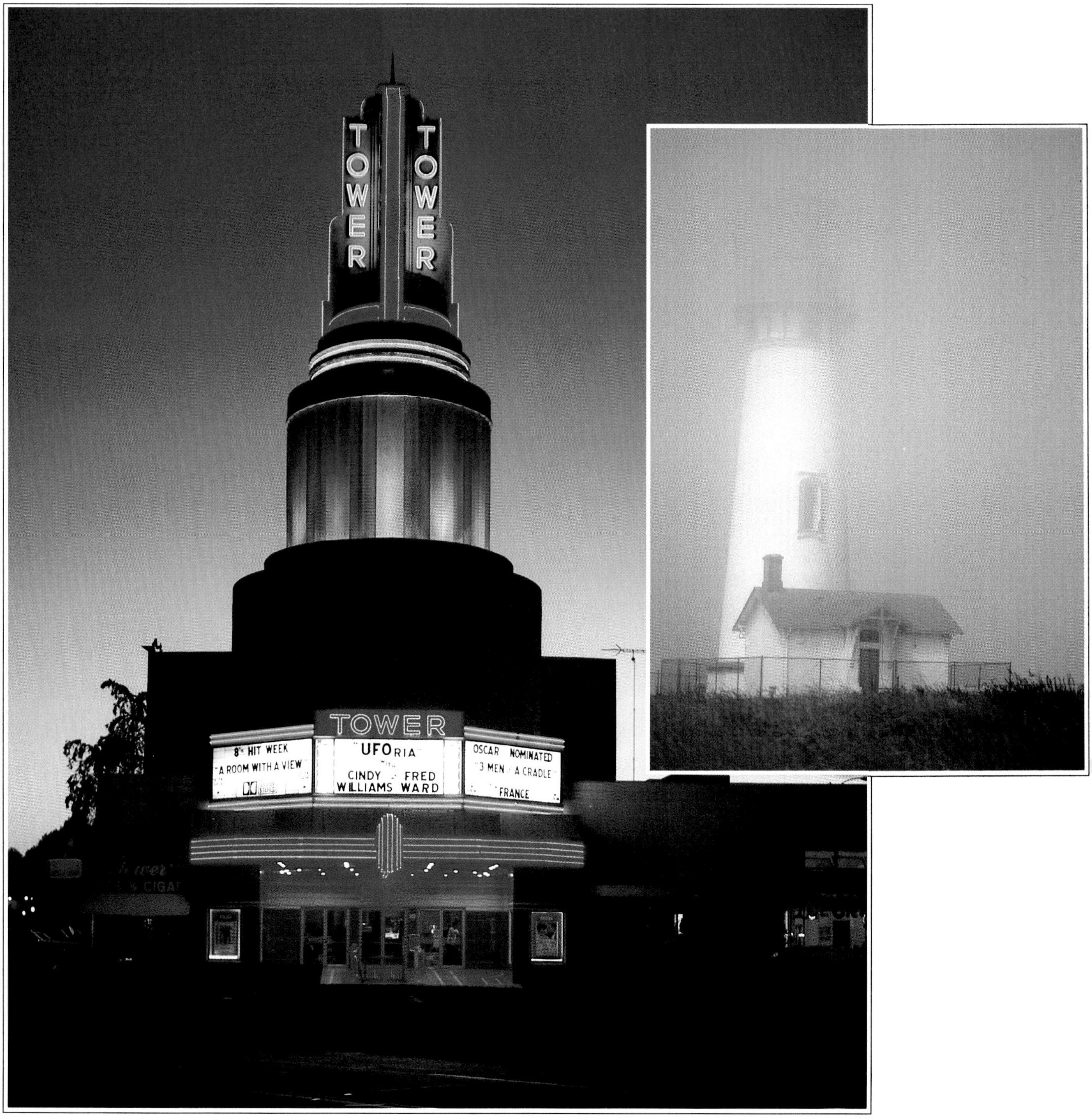
TOWER
TOWER
TOWER
8th HIT WEEK
A ROOM WITH A VIEW
UFOria
CINDY FRED
WILLIAMS WARD
OSCAR NOMINATED
3 MEN A CRADLE
FRANCE

LARGE
GRADE A
EGGS

LIBERTY•MARKET
LIBERTY•MARKET

Cast of Characters

Photo Credits

Front jacket: Wheat field © Orion Press/Stock Imagery; Child at parade, Mother and child © Terry Wild; Couple © Skjold/Photographs; Fireman © Kay Chernush/The Image Bank.

Back jacket: Woman in red hat, Mill workers © Terry Wild; Indian, Eskimo © Mark Gibson; Teens under umbrella © Martin R. Jones/Unicorn Stock Photos; Waitress © Carl Purcell; Man with lobsters © Ivan Massar/PHOTO/NATS; Office workers © Alvis Upitis/The Image Bank.

Frontispiece: Red barn, Minnesota © Bob Firth.

The Land

Pages 10, 11: Yellowdomes, remains of ancient seabed, Badlands National Park, South Dakota © Kirkendall/Spring.

Page 12: Harbor at Corea, Maine, Autumn colors, Hiawatha National Forest, Michigan © Bill Engel.

Page 13: Lighthouse on Lake Superior © Bob Firth; Magnolia Gardens, Charleston, South Carolina © Bill Engel.

Page 14: Pennsylvania farm © Terry Wild; Cape Kiwanda State Park, Oregon © Kirkendall/Spring.

Page 15: Thor's Hammer, Bryce Canyon National Park, Utah © Kirkendall/Spring.

Page 16: Mississippi River © Bob Firth.

Page 17: Mountain lake, Glacier National Park, Montana © Joe Viesti.

Pages 18, 19: Farm in fog, Hudson River Valley, New York © Joe Viesti.

Page 20: Old shack outside Abilene, Texas © Bob Daemmrich; Owens Lakebed and Sierra Nevada Mountains © Charlie Borland/Wild Vision.

Page 21: Ranching center, Lubbock, Texas © Joe Viesti.

Heritage & Faith

Page 38: Lady with rosary © Howard Zehr/Photo Agora.

Page 39: Baptism © Betts Anderson/Unicorn Stock Photos; Judge and children saluting flag © Bob Daemmrich.

Page 40: Choir © Terry Wild; Iwo Jima Memorial © Mark Antman/The Image Works.

Page 41: Martha-Mary Chapel, Sudbury, Massachusetts © Nancy Freshour.

Page 42: Statue of young Abe Lincoln, Chicago © Bill Engel.

Page 43: Painted barn, Michigan © Joe Viesti; Voting booth © Bob Daemmrich.

Pages 44, 45: Veterans Day parade © Bill Engel.

Page 46: Nuns kneeling in prayer © Bob Daemmrich; Boys lighting menorah © Zev Radovan.

Page 47: Old German Baptists, Savona, Ohio © Mark Gibson.

Page 48: First geological field trip in Oklahoma, August 1900 © PhotoEdit.

Page 49: Woman on porch © Terry Wild; Statue of Tom Sawyer and Huck Finn, Hannibal, Missouri © Bill Engel.

Page 50: Couple renewing vows on Golden Anniversary © Don and Pat Valenti/Tom Stack & Associates; Women in church © David & Linda Phillips.

Page 51: Thanksgiving © Martin R. Jones/Unicorn Stock Photos; Bell choir © Terry Wild.

American Faces

Page 83: Grandmother and granddaughter © Garry Adams/Stock Imagery.

Page 84: Toast of apples © Vasco Martin, Jr./Unicorn Stock Photos; Mother and child © Jim Bradshaw; Clown © Betts Anderson/Unicorn Stock Photos.

Page 85: Man with guitar © D. Michael Hostetler/Photo Agora; Family © David Stone/Berg & Associates; Muddy couple © Susan Gibler/Tom Stack & Associates.

Page 86: Construction worker © Mark Gibson; Welder © Terry Wild.

Page 87: Retiree in park © Terry Wild; Indian boy, Quapaw Festival, Oklahoma © Joe Viesti; Children under umbrella © James M. Mejuto.

Pages 88, 89: Hoosier farmer at Guilford Covered Bridge © Bill Thomas/PhotoEdit.

Page 89: Old cowboy © Sally Brown/Stock Imagery; Young cowboy © Dick Upchurch/Stock Imagery; Armadillo trainer © Bob Daemmrich.

Page 90: Girls © Betts Anderson/Unicorn Stock Photos; Runner © Terry Wild; Man with cigar © Carl Purcell; Teens by lockers © Karen Holsinger Mullen/Unicorn Stock Photos.

Page 91: Dancer at Fiesta de Sante Fe © Michael Heller.

Page 92: Kids with Popsicles © Terry Wild; Father and child © Jean S. Buldain/Berg & Associates; Mennonite woman © Terry Wild.

Page 93: Women at medical center © Terry Wild; Cherry Blossom Princess © Mark Gibson; Beekeeper © Rob Outlaw.

Americans at Work

Pages 116, 117: Firemen © M.L. Dembinsky, Jr., Photography Associates.

Page 118: Woman working in restaurant © Carol Kitman; Nurse with patient © Terry Wild.

Page 119; Construction surveyor © Greg Vaughn/Tom Stack & Associates.

Page 120: Man building banjo © Karen Holsinger Mullen/ Unicorn Stock Photos.

Page 121: Machinist © Terry Wild; Telephone linemen © Wardene Weisser/Berg & Associates.

Page 122: Fruit stand vendor © Terry Wild; Woman with garlic © Scott Blackman/Tom Stack & Associates.

Pages 122, 123: Cranberry harvesting crew © Michael Goodman/PHOTO/NATS.

Page 124: Doctors © National Medical Enterprises/ PhotoEdit; Priest © Terry Wild.

Page 125: Teacher and students © David Brownell; Cellist © Mark Gibson; Doctor © Gary Bublitz/M.L. Dembinsky, Jr., Photography Associates.

Page 126: Artist © Terry Wild; Man building log house © Janis Miglavs; Soldiers © Bill Engel.

Page 127: Teacher © Terry Wild; Blacksmiths shoeing horse © David & Linda Phillips.

Page 128: Construction worker © Mark Gibson; Man at computer © Gary Bublitz/M.L. Dembinsky, Jr., Photography Associates.

Page 129: Migrant workers picking tomatoes © Mark Gibson.

Page 130: Woman working in restaurant © Carol Kitman; Construction worker © Jon Feingersh/Stock Imagery.

Page 131: Paint manufacturing © Terry Wild; Street vendor © Mark Gibson.

Page 132: Union picket line © Mark Richards/PhotoEdit; Man sending Morse code © David & Linda Phillips.

Pages 132, 133: Topping off One Beacon Street, Boston © Ulrike Welsch.

Americans at Play

Page 163: Sailing © Randy James.

Page 164: Father and children at beach © Karen Holsinger Mullen/Unicorn Stock Photos; Arm wrestling © Mark Gibson.

Page 165: Tug of war © Len Berger/Berg & Associates; Swanee River Cloggers © David & Linda Phillips.

Page 166: Clown and children © Gail Denham; Artist © Bill Thomas/PhotoEdit; Special Olympics run © Judy White/Berg & Associates.

Page 167: Sledding © Max Hockemeier/Unicorn Stock Photos; Children on picnic © Karen Holsinger Mullen/ Unicorn Stock Photos; Teens playing Trivial Pursuit © Deneve Feigh Bunde/Unicorn Stock Photos.

Page 168: Children in tube castle © James M. Mejuto; Sandcastles © Margaret C. Berg/Berg & Associates; Exercise class © David & Linda Phillips; Air balloon race © Bill Engel.

Page 169: Baseball pitcher © Mark Gibson; Marathon finishers © Greg Vaughn.

Pages 170, 171: Fishing © Skjold/Photographs.

Page 171: Hang gliding © David Stone/Berg & Associates; Soccer game © Greg Vaughn; Bicycle race © Rich Turner.

Page 172: Long jump © Mark Gibson; Harmonica player © Terry Wild.

Page 173: Jazz band, Swim meet © Mark Gibson; Family camping © Team Russell/Stock Imagery.

Page 174: Man grooming dog for show, Girl playing tetherball, Lawn bowling © Mark Gibson.

Page 175: Children on slide at amusement park © Cy Furlan; Band, Dog sled race © Mark Gibson; People riding model train © David & Linda Phillips.

Pages 176, 177: Senior citizens playing chess © Greg Vaughn.

American Scenes & Celebrations

Page 208: Statue of Liberty and World Trade Center, New York City © Joe Viesti.

Page 209: Graduation © Terry Wild; Wedding © Alexander Lepeley.

Page 210: High school prom © Chris Brown/Unicorn Stock Photos; Eating at McDonald's © Alan Oddie/ PhotoEdit.

Page 211: Tall ships and sailboats off Newport, Rhode Island © Joe Viesti; Uncle Sam at Fourth of July parade © Greg Vaughn.

Pages 212, 213: Skyline of Dallas © Joe Viesti.

Page 214: Tower Theatre, Sacramento, California © George Elich; Lighthouse on Oregon coast © Bill Engel.

Page 215: Coloring Easter eggs © Greg Vaughn; Rosedown Plantation, New Orleans © Bill Engel; Fiesta de Sante Fe, New Mexico © Michael Heller.

Page 216: Birthday © Gail Denham; Cherry Blossom parade © Mark Gibson.

Page 217: Country store, Vermont © Ivan Massar/PHOTO/NATS; Shopping mall © Robert Brenner/PhotoEdit.

Page 218: Christmas tree © Brenda Matthiesen/Unicorn Stock Photos; Farm in snow © Bill Engel.

Page 219: Windmill, Colorado © Ray Richardson/Stock Imagery.

Page 224: "Our Flag Was Still There" © Bill Engel.